STAIRWAY TO
COLLEGE HEAVEN

The Most Readable
College Guide on Earth

Victoria Tillson Evans
Jonathan Perkins
Phil Sung

Published by:
Jonathan Perkins
3015 Kashiwa Street
Torrance, CA 90505

ISBN: 978-0-692-08272-0

Cover design: Norangela Bevilacqua Romero
Book design: Carla Green, Clarity Designworks

Printed in the United States of America

Contents

Acknowledgments

Victoria I'd like to thank my husband, Daniel Evans, for not only giving encouraging feedback on the text, but for his enthusiasm about the project in general. I'd also like to thank my mom, Carol Tillson, for reading each version and providing her insight. Many thanks are also due to Bethany Benitez, Deborah Phillips, and Nora Lessersohn, who all helped confirm or reshape my ideas by reading the book in its close-to-finished phase. Finally, thank you Jon and Phil for all of the work that you did to keep the book going in your individual ways.

Phil For giving me every educational opportunity and instilling in me a love of learning, I thank my parents. I'd like to give a shout out to all my hardworking current and former students and their families — I think we have learned much from each other. Future obligations go out to counselors, teachers, and parents who take a chance on us and read this thing. Thank you to my co-author Victoria and her much needed fresh perspective (sorry, Jon). And lastly, much gratitude to my wingman and sparring partner, Jon, without whose encouragement (some would say hounding) this project would never have come to fruition.

Jon Thank you to my wife, Christa Hu, for your unwavering belief that we could pull this off and for your practical advice across dozens of drafts about what was working and what wasn't. Thank you to my mom, Ellen Perkins, for using your college counseling experience to identify places where we could make our advice more nuanced and accurate. Thank you to my dad, Fraser Perkins, and my sister, Molly Perkins, for your thoughtful and amusing comments. Thank you to Norangela Bevilacqua Romero for inspiring us with your cover design. I would echo Phil's thank you to our readers; whenever writing became tedious, I found my motivation in the possibility (and, hopefully, the reality) that we could write something to make parents feel less stressed and more confident about helping their kids apply to college. Thank you to Phil for contributing your test prep expertise, for emphasizing readability over and over, and, most importantly, for your loyal friendship. Last but not least, thank you to Victoria for taking the leap of faith to collaborate on this book. What started out as a project to expand an article you had written ("ACE IT!") evolved into a grueling, 15-month ascent up the Stairway. We made it!

Yes, there are two paths you can go by, but in the long run
There's still time to change the road you're on...

-Led Zeppelin, "Stairway to Heaven."

Note to Our Readers

Throughout this book, we have chosen to capitalize key terms. If you ever forget what a capitalized term means, just check the Glossary and Resources section at the end of the book. See you on the Stairway!

— Victoria, Jon, and Phil

Prologue

Once upon a time, in a household not very far away, a mom, Michelle, lived more or less happily with her 17-year-old son, Jack. Michelle handled her parental responsibilities with occasional wisdom, some cunning, and sporadic aplomb.

One day, Jack came home from school and announced, "Mom, my counselor told me I need to start thinking about college. We got this handout with important dates and deadlines." Jack gave the piece of paper to Michelle. "Can you help me?"

Michelle froze, but only for a second. Then she nodded and rubbed her son's shoulders. "It's OK, sweetie. I've got this."

Jack disappeared upstairs, and Michelle took a quick look around the family room. She had the radio on, as usual, playing her favorite classic rock station. Where was that college book she had bought last summer? Definitely not in Jack's room. Probably collecting dust on her bookshelf upstairs.

Michelle skimmed the college handout from Jack's school counselor as she crossed the family room to the stairway. As she started up the stairs, her right foot slipped, and she rolled her ankle. She grabbed the wrought-iron railing to steady herself, but the pain shooting up her leg was so intense that she lost consciousness. "No time for this now… must help Jack get into college!" were her final thoughts as she crumpled to the floor. The college handout slipped from her hand and came to rest on the floor beside her.

Though Michelle's body was still, her mind was moving. In her dream world, she stood alone on a giant slab of dark gray rock, shrouded in fog. As she stared into the haze, she could see the silhouettes of three figures. Michelle ventured closer. The figures were chatting.

"Well, here we are again, back at work!" said the first figure, a woman.

"I can't wait to get back up to College Heaven, though," the second figure said. "Do you think we'll finish early today?"

"You never know how long it will take," the third figure said. "But I sure am looking forward to more *carne asada* nachos once we get there."

"You really can't find better nachos anywhere else," the first figure said. "I hope this next parent isn't too unrealistic, though."

"Remember that one mom who insisted that her kid apply only to Ivy League schools because he was 'too good' for anything else?" the second figure asked.

"Or the dad who called two days before the Harvard application deadline and offered to pay us to write his daughter's application essays?" the third figure asked.

"All parents are a little intense when it comes to getting their kids into college," the first figure said. "But not all parents are ready to be helped."

Michelle eavesdropped in silence. She wasn't sure about the nachos talk, but her ears were tickled at the mention of College Heaven. She made her way forward toward the three figures. The fog thinned as she drew nearer, and she saw that the figures were wearing white robes, like the kind one would find on children in a Nativity play. The figures stood at the base of an immense staircase.

"Hello?" Michelle asked, approaching the figures. "Can you help me?"

"Of course!" one of the figures, a woman, responded. "What can we do for you?"

"I'm Michelle," she said. "I was just talking to my son Jack about college, and then I think I sprained my ankle going up the stairs. Now I'm here, which is… where am I, exactly?"

"You're right where you need to be," the robed woman said, stepping forward and offering a hug. "I'm Victoria. And your ankle seems fine now!" Michelle looked down and moved her foot around in a circle. Victoria was right. It didn't hurt anymore.

"You're here because you want to get to College Heaven," the second figure said, extending his arm for a handshake. "I'm Phil."

"So this isn't College Heaven?" Michelle asked.

"Not quite, but this is the stairway to get you there," the third figure said, gesturing toward the towering stairway behind them. "And we're here to guide you there. I'm Jon, by the way." Jon gave Michelle a smile and a thumbs-up.

"But what is College Heaven, anyway?" Michelle asked.

"It's that peaceful, easy feeling parents have when they understand how applying to college works," Jon said.

"The more you know about applying to college, the less stressed you'll be," Phil said.

"And the less stressed you are, the less stressed your kid will be," Victoria said. "What did you say his name was?"

"Jack," Michelle said.

"Got it," Jon said. "Jack's college planning is a big deal, but that doesn't mean every step has to be miserable."

"So this stairway…?" Michelle asked, waving at the stairway behind the three figures, and gazing upward.

"…takes parents straight to College Heaven," Phil said.

"At first, the Boss had an escalator instead of a stairway," Jon said. "Then she realized the parents were just riding up without learning anything. There's something about the agony of climbing a stairway that really gets people's attention."

"Plus 'Stairway to College Heaven' is way catchier than 'Escalator to College Heaven,'" Victoria said.

"So I just walk on up?" Michelle asked, keeping her eyes fixed on the stairway.

"There are some tricks and traps along the way, but that's what we're here to help with," Victoria said.

"No offense," Michelle said, turning her eyes back to Victoria, Phil, and Jon, "but this is all a bit strange. These stairs. The three of you. College Heaven. How do I know I can trust you?"

"It would be strange if you didn't ask us that question," Jon said. "I have a BA in English from Stanford and a JD from Harvard. I've helped over 100 families with the college application process, and this is something I've been doing since 2011."

"I have a BA in the History of Art from Johns Hopkins and an AM and PhD in Romance Languages and Literatures from Harvard," Victoria said. "I was a professor before entering college consulting in 2013, when Jon and I met during college counseling courses through UC Irvine. I've also helped over 100 families with the college application process."

"I met Jon at Stanford, where I also got a BA in English," Phil said. "My background is a little different, though. I've worked as an ACT and SAT tutor since 1999, and over the years I've helped over 200 students successfully prep for those tests. In 2014, I began working as a college counselor, too."

"Do you mind telling me about where your students have gotten in?" Michelle asked.

"That's another question that would be strange for you not to ask," Jon said. "At the same time, we have to point out that each student's circumstances are unique."

"Of course," Michelle said.

"The short answer is that each of us has had students get in at every type of school imaginable," Victoria said, "from highly selective schools such as Harvard, Yale, Princeton, and Stanford to selective public schools such as UC Berkeley, Michigan, and Virginia to less selective colleges across the country."

"No matter what kind of student Jack is or what kind of colleges he's aiming for, the steps to get there are the same," Phil said.

"The Boss put us on stairway duty because she knows how busy parents like you are," Jon said.

"Helping you is just part of our job as College Fates," Victoria said.

"College Fates?" Michelle asked, raising her eyebrows. "That's your official job title?"

"Don't get us wrong," Jon said. "It's not like we decide anyone's college fate. But we teach you what you need to know so you can take your kid's college fate into your own hands."

"You're sure I can't just google all this stuff?" Michelle asked.

"Try," Jon said.

Michelle pulled out her iPhone. "Noooo!" she cried out. "No service!"

"Don't worry," Phil said. "Even if you could google everything right this second, it's not the best way to get started," Phil said. "That would be like trying to learn Russian by reading *Crime and Punishment* in Russian. Sure, you could do it, but it would take you an hour to understand the grammar and vocabulary of the first two sentences. Learning a new language is faster once you understand the fundamentals."

"Before you start googling college topics, we want you to understand all the important concepts," Jon said. "Once you know the big ideas, you'll be able to figure out for yourself which details matter and which don't. Then you won't get distracted by useless details."

"So what do you say?" Victoria asked. "What if we help you get to College Heaven so you can help Jack?"

"He's a bit of a procrastinator," Michelle said.

"Don't worry. We deal with that all the time," Victoria said.

"And if you let us help you, you'll be doing us a favor by giving us a chance to work off that last plate of nachos we ate," Phil said. "What do you think?"

Despite their unusual obsession with nachos, the three College Fates seemed like a better option than going the stairway alone. What did she have to lose?

"I'm in!" Michelle said. "Let's do this."

"I hope you brought comfortable shoes," Victoria said.

The fog on the stairway lifted. A light at the top of the stairway shone down like the sun upon the towering flight of stairs.

"This is where your journey of 10,000 steps begins," Phil said. "This is the Stairway to College Heaven."

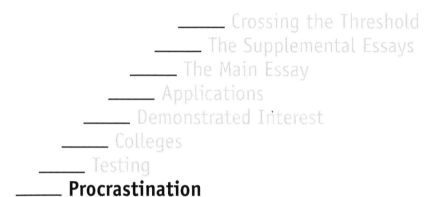
_____ **Procrastination**

"Shall we?" Jon asked Michelle as he made a sweeping gesture with his arm toward the stairs.

"We just start walking?" Michelle asked.

"Walking beats waiting," Phil said. "You know what they say: 'The first step is always the hardest.'"

Michelle began climbing the stairs, and the three College Fates trailed close behind.

"So Jack likes to procrastinate?" Victoria asked.

"Everything is last-minute with that boy," Michelle said. "He gets his work done, but it's always a scramble."

"That's pretty normal," Jon said. "One of my students, Brian, always responded the same way whenever I asked him to work on his applications or his essays: 'Sounds like a future Brian problem… Forget that guy!' He was mostly joking, but many students take what you could call a leisurely approach."

"I tell parents that kids overestimate how much they can accomplish in a few days," Phil said. "Though in all fairness, parents underestimate how much their kid can accomplish in a year."

"Applying to college is stressful enough already," Victoria said. "You don't need to add to that stress by procrastinating."

"You guys must have some fix, then, right?" Michelle asked. "I mean some way of making sure students don't procrastinate."

"Usually," Victoria said. "It depends on why the student is procrastinating."

"A lot of times, it's because the student is so busy that college planning slips to the bottom of the list," Jon said. "If the kid is loading up on AP classes and extracurricular activities, the only time left might be after midnight, which isn't really when most people are thinking to themselves, 'Hey, let's talk college planning!'"

"I've seen this with seniors and their college applications, too," Phil said. "They know they need to work ahead on their essays to get their apps in on time, but then they fall behind because of a midterm, because of a project, or because they have to be out of town for the weekend for debate or for soccer."

"Each of these decisions makes sense on its own," Victoria said. "Of course students are busy. But taken together, these decisions de-prioritize college planning."

"What's the use of doing all these great things outside of class but never investing the time to find the right colleges or do a good job on the applications?" Jon asked. "A student who has done all the academics and extracurriculars but is too busy to find time to plan for college is like someone who has a winning $100,000,000 lottery ticket but never cashes it in because he is too busy working his nine-to-five. It's just baffling."

"What do you want me to do about it, though?" Michelle asked. "I can't tell Jack to stop studying or to stop his extracurriculars."

"True," Victoria said, "but you can build college planning into your family routine. It can be as simple as saying that family dinner on the first Sunday of every month will include some college planning talk."

"Starting this routine early in high school signals that college planning is important," Jon said. "The college conversations are easy to have early on, when the stakes are low."

"Once your family commits to investing time into the college planning process, then you've already solved the biggest cause of procrastination, which is simply failing to acknowledge that a problem exists," Phil said. "By meeting together, you're saying, 'We need to do something!'"

"Then we can address the second cause of procrastination," Victoria said.

"Which is what?"

"It's the whole feeling of 'We need to do something, but I don't know what, so let's do nothing,'" Victoria said.

"Right," Phil said. "If you're procrastinating because you're not sure what to do next, that's something we can fix. It's just a matter of laying out the next steps."

"But if Jack is procrastinating even after he knows college planning is a must, and even after he knows the steps to take, then we're in for a rough ride," Jon said. "It's the old problem of 'you can lead a horse to water, but you can't make it drink.'"

"Oh, Jack's very motivated," Michelle said. "He has great grades, and he taught himself how to code when he was twelve."

"That doesn't mean he's motivated to work on college applications, though," Jon said. "The kids I've seen work the hardest on college applications aren't always the kids with the highest grades. They're the kids who know why they want to go to college."

"College will give Jack all sorts of opportunities to explore and then help him find a job he likes," Michelle said. "Then he can live his life and be happy."

"I know that, and you know that," Victoria said. "But not every 17-year-old gets it. You have to keep in mind that—"

"Hang on, sorry. I see a sign up there!" Michelle pointed to a diamond-shaped yellow road sign that was welded to the Stairway's wrought-iron handrail. The black, all-caps typeface read, "DRAGON XING."

"It just says 'Dragon Crossing,'" Phil said, shrugging his shoulders.

"A dragon? Seriously?" Michelle asked.

"Maybe we should have mentioned that earlier," Jon said.

"Yeah, you think?" Michelle asked, coming to a stop.

"It's fine. We've gone 272 days without losing a parent," Victoria said.

"You mean the dragon actually ate one of the parents you were supposed to be taking care of?" Michelle asked.

"Oh, no, nothing like that," Jon said. "It was just this one dad. Joe, I think his name was. He climbed for about 30 minutes and then froze. He just stood there staring up at the Stairway. No matter what we said or did, he wouldn't move. The dragon didn't know what to do with him, either, so she just picked him up and flew him back down to the bottom of the Stairway, and he just kind of wandered off, I guess. Haven't seen him since. Probably in limbo somewhere."

"So long as you keep moving, you'll be fine," Phil said.

"I really think the climb would be better without the dragon," Michelle said.

"At first, the Boss upstairs thought so, too," Jon said. "The test version of the Stairway was completely dragon-free. But you know what happened? Parents just started lounging around and chatting. Too much lollygagging and not enough climbing. Instead of learning about applying to college, the parents were procrastinating!"

"Not exactly a surprise that their own kids would procrastinate on college applications, too," Victoria said. "The apple doesn't fall far from the tree."

"That's why the Boss added a dragon," Phil said. "She even gave the dragon a nickname: Draggin. As in, 'You're draggin' your you-know-what.' The Boss believed being chased by a dragon would make parents climb a little faster."

"She's not wrong," Victoria said. "Not that she usually is. Stick close, and we'll keep you out of Draggin's way."

"Doesn't look like I have much of a choice," Michelle said. "It's either wait for Draggin to catch me or keep climbing."

"Knowing your enemy is a good thing," Jon said. "So many parents want to rush into the logistics of figuring out where to apply or how to write the application essays that they forget the biggest obstacle of all: procrastination."

"I get that," Michelle said, "but then shouldn't you be talking to Jack instead of me?"

"It's like when you're flying and there's a drop in cabin pressure," Phil said. "First put on your own oxygen mask and then help your child."

"Let's be real," Victoria said. "You're the one who's going to be buying all the books about applying to college." Michelle nodded, remembering the dozens of unread college books lining her bookshelf. "You're not going to tell Jack to figure it out and then sit back and hope for the best."

"I've had families try this, and it never works out," Phil said.

"Procrastination is the deadliest college application sin," Jon said as the group passed by a small sign that read, "College Heaven: 9,901 Steps." "We've already done 99 steps, and it's only been three minutes."

"Then let's keep climbing!" Michelle said.

"That's the spirit!" Victoria said.

Words of Wisdom from the Boss

"I like the old proverb that says, 'The best time to plant a tree was 20 years ago. The second-best time is now.' College planning takes more time than you might expect, so stop procrastinating. Getting started is as easy as scheduling a time when you and your child can sit down in a relaxed setting to talk about college goals."

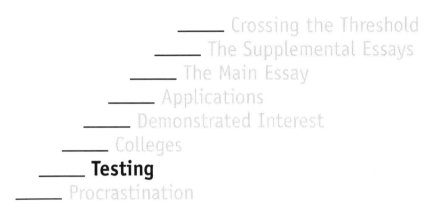
"There's so much information about the college application process," Michelle said as the group slowly marched together up the stairs. "Jack's only a junior, so I know we have time, but where do I even begin?"

"Standardized testing," Phil said. "No question. That's a big item that requires months of lead time."

"You mean the SAT?" Michelle asked.

"Or the ACT," Victoria said.

"What's the difference?" Michelle asked. "And how do we figure out which one Jack should take?"

The group reached a landing in the Stairway, and the Stairway split into two parallel sets of stairs, both with wrought-iron railings, separated by a gap of about three feet.

ACT vs. SAT

"You and I will take the stairs on the left," Jon said to Michelle as he pointed to the left, walked toward the left-hand side, and began to climb the stairs. Michelle followed close behind.

"We'll take the stairs on the right," Phil said as he and Victoria headed toward the right-hand side and started up the stairs, across the way from Jon and Michelle.

"Like these stairs, the ACT and the SAT take you to the same place," Jon said. "Colleges accept both. They don't prefer one over the other."

"Both have math through Algebra 2, along with reading comprehension, grammar, and an optional essay," Victoria said across the gap.

"Which isn't really optional at all," Jon said.

"That doesn't make any sense," Michelle said. "How can the writing section of the ACT or SAT be optional and not optional?"

"Technically, it's optional," Victoria said, "meaning you can choose to take the ACT or SAT without the essay. But practically speaking, it's not optional because many schools require it. So always sign up for the writing section!"

"Math, reading comprehension, grammar, and the essay are all features the ACT and SAT have in common," Phil said, "but one difference is that the ACT has a science section that asks students to interpret data from charts, graphics, and tables."

"Does that really matter for most students?" Michelle asked.

"Though you don't need specific science knowledge to do well on the ACT, sometimes students who like science score higher on the ACT," Victoria said.

"I had a student who spent a year focusing on the SAT before the parents got in touch with me," Phil said. "I told him to try the ACT, and he got a perfect score. He's a computer science major now."

"Jack likes science, but I don't want to guess. I want to know for sure that he's taking the right test," Michelle said.

"Then he'll have to take some practice exams," Victoria said. "Taking the PSAT or the PreACT sophomore or junior year at his school is one way."

"Talk to his high school college counselor for more information because scheduling for those tests is done through the high school," Jon said.

"But do it before October of junior year," Phil said. "That will be Jack's last chance to take these tests."

"Another option is taking a sample ACT from the ACT website or a sample SAT from the College Board website," Jon said.

"Wait, should I be writing these websites down?" Michelle asked. "I don't want to forget about them later."

"No need," Victoria said. "When you get to the top of the Stairway, we'll make sure you get a cheat sheet with links and other resources to help you keep Jack on track."

"Perfect," Michelle said, turning from Victoria back to Phil. "You were saying Jack can take sample ACT or sample SAT tests, but if he's supposed to do that on his own, I'm not sure it will happen. What other options do we have?"

"If Jack needs more structure — and most students do — you can try getting in touch with Test Prep companies," Phil said. "Many of them offer free diagnostic tests."

"Sitting for an actual exam without taking at least one timed practice test is a big mistake!" Victoria said. "That's like trying to do a back handspring without any training. No matter how much natural acrobatic talent you have, you're not going to land on your feet the first time."

"I've had smart kids who didn't take practice tests mess up on the real thing because they couldn't manage their time," Phil said. "One of my students panicked the first time she took her first real SAT. She didn't finish a few sections because she allowed herself to get stuck on tough questions in the middle of the test. Except for the math, the questions aren't in order of difficulty, so getting bogged down in the middle of a section and not even seeing all the questions is disastrous. She took practice tests before her second attempt and scored 200 points better."

"But the SAT and ACT are scored differently, right?" Michelle asked. "So how do I know which one Jack did better on?"

"The maximum score is 36 for the ACT and 1600 for the SAT," Phil said. "To see which score is higher, google 'SAT ACT concordance.' If Jack scores higher on one of them, he should go with that one. But if Jack scores at about the same percentile on both tests, then he should prep for whichever one feels more comfortable."

Jon and Michelle's stairs on the left now merged with Phil and Victoria's stairs on the right, and the group again found itself on a large landing. "So both the ACT and the SAT take students to the same place," Michelle said.

"Exactly," Phil said. "And once you have an idea about which test Jack will take, you can start thinking about Test Prep."

Test Prep

"Does Test Prep even work?" Michelle asked.

"Test-taking is a skill that improves with practice, just like playing a sport or a musical instrument," Victoria said.

"So those companies that guarantee score increases of 200 points can actually deliver?" Michelle asked.

"In my experience, 100 points on the SAT or 4 points on the ACT is more realistic," Phil said. "But there are some caveats. It's easier to go from a 1200 to a 1300 than from a 1500 to a 1600."

"So going from nearly perfect to perfect is harder than going from pretty good to good," Michelle said. "Makes sense."

"Right," Phil said. "Also, some sections of the tests are more coachable than others. Grammar is usually the easiest section to improve, then math. Reading comprehension is the hardest. It's just very difficult to become a strong reader in a short period of time."

"Reading is really that hard?" Michelle asked.

"I had one student who got perfect grammar and math scores after two lessons with me but labored for a year without getting a perfect on reading comp," Phil said. "That's why high reading scores are more impressive than high math scores."

"How long will it take a student to fully prep for the SAT or ACT?" Michelle asked.

"100 hours," Phil said.

"Whoa, 100 hours?" Michelle asked.

"That includes classes, homework, and practice tests," Phil said.

"Are you kidding me?" Michelle asked. "There's no way Jack has time for that." Michelle's comment was met with a thunderous roar from below. "What was that?"

"That's just Draggin," Phil said. "Test Prep is not a great thing to procrastinate on!"

"Of course Jack can't do 100 hours of Test Prep in one month," Jon said, "but he can also spread that prep time out."

"Schedule the tests first, and start prepping a few months before the test date," Phil said.

"If Jack has any documented disabilities, such as a learning disability or a physical impairment, remember to request a testing accommodation," Victoria said. "That might mean extra time for the test or being able to type out the essay portion instead of writing it by hand."

"Getting approved for an accommodation can take two months or more, so start the process as early as possible," Jon said.

"Jack doesn't have any disabilities," Michelle said. "But that leads me to another question: when should Jack take the SAT or ACT?"

"Fall of junior year is ideal for most students to take the test for the first time," Jon said. "That means doing some Test Prep over the summer after sophomore year."

"When Jack should start Test Prep depends on what his PSAT or PreACT score is and on how much he is trying to improve," Phil said. "Talk to your college counselor to make sure you have a plan that makes sense."

"Wait," Michelle said, turning to Jon. "You said fall of junior year is a good time to take the test for the first time. So it's OK to take the SAT or ACT more than once?"

"Two times is good," Phil said. "No more than three times. Diminishing returns after that point."

"Three sounds like a lot," Michelle said. "And I don't even know what kind of Test Prep options are out there."

At that moment, the group heard a murmur of voices from above on the Stairway, and a man dressed in a suit popped into view. In his hand, he held a stick to which was attached a purple triangular flag with the words "HEAVENCORP TOURS" written in white.

"Who are they?" Michelle asked the three College Fates, lowering her voice.

"Oh, that's just HeavenCorp," Jon said as the tour guide droned on, leading his group down toward Michelle and the three College Fates. "They run tours to College Heaven. Sister company of TestCorp, a national Test Prep outfit."

"But they're going the wrong way!" Michelle said. "Shouldn't they be going up, and not down?"

"It's the same with Test Prep in a big group setting," Jon said. "It's cheaper, but it takes a bit longer."

"This HeavenCorp tour left two days ago, but it's sort of a 1,000 steps up, 900 steps down kind of deal," Phil said.

"You're not really a fan of Test Prep classes, I see," Michelle said.

"See all those people in the tour group staring off into space?" Phil asked. The HeavenCorp tour guide had led his group farther down the Stairway, where he was lecturing about the intricate *fleur-de-lis* ironwork in the railing as the members of his tour stared up at the clouds. "I used to teach classes for TestCorp. The problem is that these classes typically teach to the middle. Advanced kids get bored, and beginners get lost because TestCorp can't customize to every student."

"And they are wildly inefficient with time because they can't skip over concepts your child already knows," Victoria said. "Three-hour classes are common."

"I've had classes with non-native English speakers mixed in with students who were scoring in the mid-600s in the reading section," said Phil. "On the math side, the scores ranged from 500 to 700. It's impossible to be efficient. Students don't want to ask questions because they're afraid they'll look dumb or slow down the class. It's tough on the teacher and on the students."

"Not to mention that you have no idea what kind of teacher you're going to get," Jon said. Michelle and the three College Fates watched the HeavenCorp tour disappear into the fog that covered the Stairway below them.

"As far as teachers go, you want to look for experience," Phil said as the group resumed its climb up the Stairway. "That's the most important factor in a teacher. I've subbed for classes that had teachers straight out of training, and more often than not, the students hadn't learned what they should have. New teachers focus on delivering all the info they're supposed to. Experienced teachers focus on making the crucial info stick."

"If I don't find a Test Prep class for Jack, what else can I do?" Michelle asked. The group arrived at another landing in the Stairway, this one equipped with a comfy couch. On the couch lay a parent who had dozed off, apparently while trying to educate himself about college admissions, judging from the fact that he was now using a three-inch-thick copy of *American News and Earth Report*'s *300 Best Colleges in the Entire Universe* as a pillow.

"That guy can't catch a break," Jon said.

"You know him?" Michelle asked.

"Well, I haven't exactly spoken to him yet," Victoria said. "He's been on that couch for at least the past week. He can't seem to make progress."

"That's what I see with Test Prep, too," Phil said. "Some parents figure that the information is out there, so there's no point in paying for a Test Prep class or tutor. But I love what American entrepreneur Derek Sivers says: 'If information was the answer, then we'd all be billionaires with perfect abs.'"

"He has a point," Michelle said. Jon picked up the blanket that had fallen from the couch to the floor and draped it over the slumbering father. "So are you saying self-study never works?"

"Maybe not never, but rarely," Phil said. "I've seen it fail so many times. One parent reached out to me at the end of summer to help her son because his test scores weren't improving. At the first meeting, on the dining room table, was a stack of Test Prep books and college guides two feet high. The mom said these were the books her child was using to prep and that he spent two hours a day studying for the SAT and researching colleges. I flipped through the books, and they were practically unused. I don't know what the kid was doing in his room for two hours a day, but he wasn't studying. He probably read the first few pages of the first book and got overwhelmed. Or bored. Most high school kids are really bad at doing Test Prep on their own."

"I totally get buying books and never reading them," Michelle said. "I still haven't spent more than ten minutes looking at those college guides I bought."

"Accountability is hard to come by with self-study," Jon said. "The same is true for students that go into their rooms, close the doors, and later tell their parents that they were spending the whole time working on college applications. Students need to be quizzed on their progress, or else progress won't happen."

"If Jack insists on self-study, he should check out Khan Academy," Phil said. "It's free, and it's probably the best self-study option for the SAT."

"And with Khan Academy, you can ask him to show you what he's reviewed so you know he's not slacking off," Victoria said.

"But if we don't want classes or self-study, what's left?" Michelle asked.

"There's always the private tutor option," Phil said. "It's more expensive but more efficient. If it were up to me, I'd spend money on a few hours with a good private tutor before I spent it on a class."

"You're not just saying that because you're a private Test Prep tutor?" Michelle asked.

"I've told parents, 'Go ahead and try the class if you want, but you're wasting your money,'" Phil said. "This happens every year. I have parents come back to me and say, 'You were right.' In the end they end up paying for a class *and* a tutor. When I get students who have already been through a class, I always ask what they learned. Most of the time, they can't tell me a single thing. The information in the classes isn't bad. It's just not delivered effectively, and there's not enough reinforcement."

"By reinforcement, I assume you mean homework," Michelle said. "The thing is, I'm not sure Jack would do the homework. If I'm going to spend the money on a private tutor, I want to make sure he does the work."

"That's so true," Jon said. "It's the same thing with college counseling. You reap what you sow, or however you want to put it."

"The student has to want it," Victoria said, "or else your money won't go as far as you hope."

"Once when Phil and I were discussing whether Test Prep and college counseling are worth it, he told me, 'Just look at whether the kid studies hard, and you'll know,'" Jon said. "I think he's right. If a student takes initiative and tries hard, he'll get a lot out of working closely with a Test Prep tutor or a college counselor. Unfortunately, the ones that most need the help are usually the least ready to receive it."

"For sure," Phil said. "I always tell parents right away that they're wasting their money if their child is unmotivated. Most parents discontinue at that point. But occasionally, well-meaning parents will continue with lessons and hope that their child miraculously starts caring. I had one student who only cared about playing football. It sounds like a cliché, but it's a true story. The kid never did homework. I'm pretty sure he would rather have been at the dentist getting a cavity filled. He just wasn't academically-minded. Eventually, the mom saw the futility and threw in the towel. The thing is, even if you stuck with it and forced your child kicking and screaming to go through Test Prep, and your child actually over-achieves and improves, do you think your child is ready to be successful at college? You have to look at the bigger picture, too. Test Prep is as good a time as any for a student to start taking ownership of his education. That's an attractive quality for college."

"That's a good point," admitted Michelle. "I know Jack cares, but he's not always the best about doing work on his own. Is Test Prep still worth it?"

"There's some grinding it out required to score in the elite level, but it's possible to raise your score without doing homework if the lesson time is used effectively," Phil said. "That's a contingency plan, not the ideal situation, though."

"Let's say Jack figures out whether to take the ACT or SAT, does his Test Prep, and takes the test a couple times," Michelle said. "What happens next?"

"We'll get into that in more detail when we talk about college applications," Victoria said, "but the short version is that you'll order score reports through the ACT or SAT website to be sent to the colleges."

Reporting ACT and SAT Scores

"Jack has to send all his test scores?" Michelle asked. "What if he messes up the first time around?"

"Each college has different policies for which test scores they require to be sent," Jon said. "It's annoying, but you'll have to check each college's website."

"Many colleges allow what is called Score Choice, meaning the student gets to decide which scores that college receives," Victoria said.

"Even if you don't use Score Choice, sending all Jack's scores won't necessarily be a negative because most colleges Superscore," Phil said.

"That means they take the best section scores from all the tests and combine them into a single score," Victoria said.

"Notable examples of schools that don't Superscore include the University of California system and University of Michigan," Jon said.

"Also, some schools that Superscore the SAT don't Superscore the ACT," Phil said.

"That seems pretty straightforward," Michelle said. "Is that it for standardized tests?"

"Well," Jon said, pausing for a second. "Almost, but not quite."

SAT Subject Tests

"Beyond the SAT and the ACT, you still have to keep track of the SAT Subject Tests," Phil said. "Those are one-hour tests on single subjects such as Biology, US History, and Spanish."

"Not every college requires them," Victoria said. "As with superscoring and Score Choice, the policies vary from school to school."

"That said, if Jack is applying anywhere as an engineering or computer science major, chances are excellent he'll have to take the Math Level 2 plus Physics, Chemistry, or Biology SAT Subject Tests," Jon said.

Michelle brought out her phone to bring up her iCalendar. "So when's a good time for the SAT Subject Tests?"

"May or June of the year the student takes the high school course for that subject," Jon said. "If Jack is taking his final exam for AP Biology in May of sophomore year, he should take the SAT Subject Test that May or

June. There's no way he should be waiting until the following fall to take the SAT Subject Test. He's never going to retain that info over the summer, and he's not going to study for it over the summer, either."

"Yeah, he'll be too busy procrastinating on the required summer reading," Phil said.

"True," Michelle said, shaking her head.

"Give Jack as much time as possible," Phil said. "I love Hofstadter's Law: it always takes longer than you expect, even when you take into account Hofstadter's Law. Students get incredibly busy with their academics, extracurriculars, and family vacations."

"Jack probably doesn't need Test Prep for SAT Subject Tests if he's taking an honors level or higher course and getting an A," Victoria said.

"He should take a practice test, though," Phil said. "The College Board publishes a book containing a practice test for all the subjects called *The Official Study Guide for All SAT Subject Tests*."

"When Jack has his scores back, he'll need to figure out which ones to report," Jon said. "Most colleges will let Jack decide. Our rule is to report any score of 700 or above."

"OK," Michelle said. "But hold on. You mentioned Jack should take the SAT Subject Test for Biology about the same time he takes the final for AP Biology. So how do AP Test scores fit into the admissions process?"

AP Tests and IB Exams

"AP Test scores don't matter much in the admissions process," Victoria said. "The same is true for scores on International Baccalaureate Exams, often referred to as IB Exams. Good AP and IB scores are like icing on the cake."

"Jack will have the option to self-report AP Test scores and IB Exam scores on his college applications, meaning he won't have to send an official score report from the testing agency when he applies," Phil said. "He'll only need to send those official reports to the school he decides to attend. High scores might get him some college credit, or they might let him test out of some intro level courses."

"If reporting these scores is up to Jack, how do we decide which scores are good enough to include in the application?" Michelle asked.

"We tell our students to report 4s and 5s on AP Tests and 6s and 7s on IB Exams," Victoria said.

"So when it comes to testing, we have the SAT, the ACT, the SAT Subject Tests, the AP Tests, and the IB Exams," Michelle said. "But they don't all carry the same weight in the admissions process."

"Right," Victoria said. "SAT and ACT scores are very important, almost as important as GPA and course rigor."

"That said, some schools are Test Optional Colleges, and neither the SAT nor the ACT is required," Jon said. "Try the FairTest website for a list of Test Optional Colleges. Still, if you're targeting Top 25 Schools or flagship public universities, Jack won't be able to escape the SAT or ACT."

"SAT Subject Test scores, AP scores, and IB scores matter much less than SAT and ACT scores," Victoria said, "but SAT Subject Test scores typically carry more weight than AP scores and IB scores. Even if a school doesn't require any SAT Subject Tests, high scores show mastery of the subjects."

While Michelle took a slow deep breath, Victoria eased up in front of a sign attached to the railing. "College Heaven: 8,842 Steps," it read. She gave a "keep-it-moving" gesture to Jon and Phil.

"That next landing is the end of the testing section of the Stairway," Phil said. "Let's take a break up there."

"That wasn't too bad," Michelle said as she continued on. "We didn't even see Draggin'!"

"See?" Victoria said. "We told you not to worry. Just keep moving, and you'll be fine!"

Words of Wisdom from the Boss

"Colleges accept either the ACT or the SAT, and your child's score on either of these tests is a significant admissions factor, right up there with GPA and course rigor. Whether your child preps for the ACT or SAT through a class, with a private tutor, or on his own, he should expect to invest 100 hours. Pick SAT Subject Tests based on your child's most advanced courses, and don't worry too much about AP Tests or IB Exams, since those matter less."

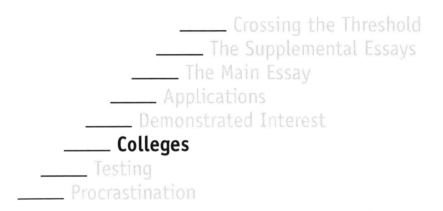

"Wait!" Michelle said. The College Fates paused on the landing. "I get that there's a lot I can do to help Jack boost his SAT or ACT score. But what's a good score?"

"Perfect timing," Phil said. "That question fits right in with figuring out where to apply to college."

"This next section of the Stairway is all about understanding how to build a good College List," Jon said.

"I've been putting that off," Michelle said. "There are thousands of colleges out there. I don't know where to start." Draggin let out a loud roar that rose up through the fog below.

"No more procrastination talk!" Victoria said. "We don't want Draggin getting any closer. Come on! We'll explain."

A Good College List

"The easiest way to answer your question about what's a good SAT or ACT score is to talk about what makes a good College List," Jon said.

"The basic strategy is to start making a good College List of Reach, Target, and Safety Schools by March of junior year," Phil said.

"What do those terms mean, exactly?" Michelle asked.

"It's pretty straightforward," Phil said. "Our rule of thumb is that any school with an acceptance rate below 25 percent is automatically a Reach School. You could even call schools with acceptance rates below 15 percent Super-Reach Schools."

"That means the Top 25 Schools are almost always Reach Schools because of their low acceptance rates," Victoria said. "Of course, there are exceptions here and there, but those are so student-specific that they're impossible to generalize."

"Also, no matter what the college's acceptance rate may be, if Jack's SAT or ACT score is below the 25th percentile for that college, it's still a Reach School," Jon said.

"To put it another way, when you see the 25th percentile score, that means a full 75 percent of successful applicants scored above that level," Phil said.

"Colleges publish SAT and ACT percentiles?" Michelle asked.

"Most release the 'mid-range' scores, meaning the range of scores that covers the 25th to 75th percentile," Phil said. "The College Board's Big Future website is an easy way to find those."

"Then a good SAT or ACT score would be one that's at or above the 75th percentile?"

"Right," Jon said. "If a college is not in the Top 25 and if Jack's SAT or ACT score is at or above the 75th percentile, that college is usually a Safety School.

"Usually?" Michelle asked.

"It often depends on the choice of major," Jon said. "When a student applies to a major that's more competitive at that particular school, the chances go down."

"Engineering, computer science, business, and biology are examples of selective majors that can shift a Safety School into the Target School category," Victoria said.

"You mentioned what happens if Jack's score is above the 75th percentile or below the 25th percentile, but what if it's in the middle of that range?" Michelle asked.

"If a school is not in the Top 25 and if Jack's score falls in that middle 25th to 75th percentile range, then it's a Target School," Phil said.

"Whenever you and Jack are discussing a college, the first thing you should do is categorize it as a Reach, Target, or Safety School," Victoria said.

"If you don't label the schools correctly, there's no way to know if you have a good College List," Phil said.

"Aim for three Reach Schools, four Target Schools, and three Safety Schools," Jon said.

"That's a reasonable approach," Victoria said. "And if you or Jack is adamant about adding Reach Schools, fine — but don't work on more Reach Schools until after he's submitted applications for at least three Safety Schools and at least four Target Schools. That way, you know he'll have some realistic options."

"Isn't it a bit simplistic to label the schools based only on SAT or ACT percentiles?" Michelle asked as the group climbed the Stairway. "What about GPA?"

"SAT and ACT percentiles are good for a back-of-the-envelope calculation," Victoria said. "Course rigor — like the number of honors and AP courses — and GPA are right up there with SAT and ACT scores as important admissions factors."

"If GPA is so important, though, then why shouldn't I use it to categorize schools for Jack?" Michelle asked.

"A 3.9 GPA at one school doesn't necessarily carry the same weight as a 3.9 GPA from a school across town," Victoria said. "When evaluating an applicant, admissions reps look at the context of the school, the school district, the state, and the country. Basically, the questions are, 'How is this student doing within the context of her school? How is she doing compared to the rest of the applicant pool?' It doesn't make sense to look at GPA without looking at context, which is why we categorize schools based on SAT or ACT scores."

"With that said, if Jack's GPA is out of sync with his ACT or SAT scores — meaning that his ACT or SAT scores are much higher than one would usually see for his GPA, or vice-versa — that's a good signal to be more conservative in categorizing colleges," Jon said. "For example, a college that's a Safety School for a student with a 34 ACT score and a 4.8 weighted GPA could be a Target School or a Reach School for a student with a 34 ACT score and a 3.8 weighted GPA."

"But when the ACT or SAT score matches the GPA, it's fine to rely on the ACT or SAT score to label a college as a Reach School, Target School, or Safety School," Phil said.

"Understood," Michelle said. "But beyond the numbers, what makes a student stand out? Lots of kids have the same GPA and test scores. My friend whose daughter is a senior told me that students have to 'pop,' especially to have a chance at Reach Schools, but I have no idea what that even means."

"We'll show you up here," Victoria replied, pointing ahead.

Hooks

As the group reached the next landing, they saw a small sign posted on a gate on the right handrail of the Stairway. It read, "HOOK HYPERLOOP," and contained a small fishhook logo. A couple dozen parents waited in a line extending from the gate, which opened into a spherical pod that measured ten feet across. The exterior of the pod gleamed white, and the interior contained black leather seats with red stitching. The pod sat at the bottom of a long tube that was bolted to the Stairway railing. The tube extended upward for as far as they could see.

"What's this Hook Hyperloop?" Michelle asked as she looked across the landing.

"It's just an easier way for some families to get to College Heaven," Victoria said.

"But what's with the name?" Michelle asked. "A Hook? I don't get it."

"A Hook is a quality or experience that a college considers especially valuable," Jon said.

"Great! Where do I get one for Jack?" Michelle asked. "Ooh, is that what that vending machine over there is for?" Before any of the three College Fates could utter a word, Michelle sprinted over to the vending machine next to the gate to the Hook Hyperloop loading area. From across the landing, the three College Fates watched Michelle try to insert a dollar bill several times, only to have the machine spit it back out. "No!" Michelle began pounding on the outside of the machine. "Come on!" she shouted as the parents waiting in line turned to stare. After giving the vending machine a vicious kick, Michelle grabbed her right toe, turned around, and limped back across the landing to the three College Fates. "The machine is broken!"

"The thing about hooks is…"

"What? What is it?" Michelle asked. "Can I buy one online? The whole vending machine thing did seem kind of antiquated, now that I think about it."

"The thing is, you can't actually buy a Hook," Jon said. "I mean, yes, once in a while someone comes along with millions of dollars to donate, but that's rare."

"Most Hooks are either things you're born with or things you work at over many years," Phil said.

"Like what?" Michelle asked.

"At the front of the line is Emmanuel's mom," Phil said. "She immigrated from Nigeria, and Emmanuel will be the first in his family to graduate from college. That means he actually has two Hooks — being a 'first gen' student and being an underrepresented minority."

"What counts as an underrepresented minority?" Michelle asked. "I don't think Jack qualifies, but he is one-fourth Hungarian."

"For the most part, it means Black or African American, Hispanic or Latino, American Indian, Alaska Native, Native Hawaiian, or Pacific Islander," Jon said. "For some schools in the Midwest, Asian American might count, but typically not for the Top 25 Schools."

"Colleges might not be fond of this distillation," Phil said. "But our intent is to describe what we've observed, not to critique the value of diversity or the methods by which colleges attempt to achieve it."

"All other things being equal, being an underrepresented minority is generally a plus factor in the admissions process," Jon said.

"Behind Emmanuel's mom is Lacey's dad," Victoria said, nodding toward the second person in line. "He graduated from Princeton, which makes Lacey a Legacy there. That's a huge plus."

"Next in line is Rohan's dad," Phil said. "Rohan built his own electric motorcycle prototype and has won prizes at numerous science competitions at the county, state, and national level. So he's one of those kids whose exceptional talent counts as a Hook."

"That's what's hard for parents to see sometimes," Jon said. "Getting great grades and SAT or ACT scores is wonderful, and so is participating in school clubs or community service. But a talent or activity that becomes a Hook is, by definition, something that students can't do *en masse*."

"Like building an electric motorcycle prototype?" Michelle asked.

"You got it," Phil said. "There really is no formula or template. Here's the question to ask yourself: 'When I see what this student has done, do I wonder how in the world a 17-year-old pulled it off?' If your answer to that question is 'yes,' then there's a great chance that colleges will see that accomplishment as a Hook."

"Behind Rohan's dad is Katy's mom," Victoria said. "Katy is the seventh-best tennis player in the US. When a student is good enough to be recruited, athletics can be another type of exceptional talent that counts as a Hook."

Michelle shook her head. "I don't think Jack has any Hooks. I mean, he does like science, but he's never built anything or won a national science prize. He plays club soccer and loves it, but he's not being recruited or anything. What does that mean?"

"It's fine," Jon said, shrugging his shoulders. "Most of our students don't have Hooks. That might put many of the Top 25 Schools out of reach, but our students still end up with plenty of choices for college."

"Hooks are rare," Phil said. "Otherwise they wouldn't be Hooks. Even for students without Hooks, it's still important that they use their time outside of class to pursue leadership opportunities and explore academic interests."

"We're not trying to discourage you," Victoria said. "We want you to understand how competitive the applicant pool is so you can help Jack be realistic about his options."

"Many parents are comparing their kids with other students at the same high school, thinking, 'My kid is in the top 10 percent at his school, so he must be competitive for an Ivy League school,'" Jon said. "But if these parents thought about the whole applicant pool, which includes kids with Hooks, they would be much more realistic."

Being Realistic

"If you don't know Jack is up against students with Hooks, it's easy to get carried away," Victoria said. "And you might end up putting unnecessary pressure on Jack."

"What do you mean?" Michelle asked.

"Take a kid who has a 4.8 weighted GPA and over a 1500 on the SAT, and who has spent countless hours volunteering at a local hospital and playing varsity soccer," Jon said. "If you're that kid's parent, you're saying to yourself, 'My kid is pretty awesome,' and you're right. Come on, a 1500 is like 98th percentile. But that doesn't mean this kid will get into an Ivy League school."

"Think about how small the incoming classes are at hyper-selective schools like Stanford," Phil said. "If the school is accepting 2,000 applicants, about half will be men, and about half will be women. There will be at least one student from every state and at least one from 50 or more countries around the world. There will be recruited athletes, Legacy students, and underrepresented minorities, which easily account for half of the incoming class. We haven't even gotten to the students who have demonstrated exceptional talent in the sciences or the arts. How many slots are left for well-rounded smart kids? Not that many."

"Brutal," Michelle said. "But you never know, right?"

"Mostly we do," Jon said. "If a student has great numbers but no Hooks, then the application essays and the Letters of Recommendation have to be stellar to have a chance at one of those super-selective schools. I'm talking about letters where the teacher says, 'This is one of the best students I've ever had.'"

"Getting into hyper-selective colleges is tough," Phil said. "That's why one of your most important jobs is to remind Jack that his potential isn't contingent on being accepted into an Ivy League school."

"That's something I have to do nearly every week," Victoria said. "I once worked with a young lady who was a straight-A student until she developed an anxiety disorder, and her grades plummeted junior year. She and her mom always thought of her as Ivy-bound, but by the summer of her senior year, I had spent multiple sessions discussing her list with both of them to explain why applying only to Top 25 Schools was a really bad idea."

"You have to be open-minded about which schools are 'good enough' for Jack," Jon said. "That universe of schools has to be broader than the Top 25 Schools. What schools did you have in mind for Jack, anyway?" Jon asked.

"Cornell, Columbia, and MIT could all be great for Jack," Michelle said. "Oh, and he really liked Northwestern when we visited."

"Where else?" Jon asked.

"I haven't gotten that far," Michelle said. "I know these schools are all long-shots, but he has worked so hard, and I want to stay positive. I was waiting until later to talk about the other schools."

As soon as Michelle uttered these words, the group heard another loud roar from below. A flash of orange glowed through the fog that still covered the lower parts of the Stairway. Then a giant purple dragon flapped into sight, spewing fire.

"Draggin!" Victoria yelled. "Quick! Up the stairs!"

Michelle and the three College Fates sprinted as fast as they could, leaping up stairs two at a time until their quads burned. They looked back down the Stairway, only to see Draggin perched on the handrail about 50 steps below.

"We're still out of range of her fireballs," Phil said. "Good thing she's more of a short-range flyer. Let's keep moving, though." The group continued its upward trek, this time at a more comfortable walking pace.

"I know you put off having this talk with Jack because you don't want to be discouraging. But it's also discouraging to get rejected from all the schools on your list."

"Don't get me wrong," Jon said. "I get that you don't want to have a painful conversation with Jack where you acknowledge that Reach Schools probably won't accept him. But we're not saying Jack shouldn't apply to any Reach Schools. We're just saying he shouldn't apply *only* to Reach Schools."

"Or mostly to Reach Schools," Victoria said. "Three Reach Schools, four Target Schools, and three Safety Schools. That's the way to do it."

"It's hard to say 'no' to our kids," Phil said. "Especially when we're talking about their futures. But being honest with Jack about his chances doesn't mean you're crushing his dreams. Kids are more resilient than their parents give them credit for."

"One of my students was relieved when his parents finally admitted that Stanford was a Reach School," Victoria said. "So relieved that he decided not to apply at all. Letting Jack know that you love and support him no matter what the outcome is an important part of this whole process."

"The whole point of researching and applying to colleges is to give Jack options," Phil said. "If you let Jack apply to eight Reach Schools and two Safety Schools because you think Jack is too good for Safety Schools, there's a high probability he'll only get into the Safety Schools, and he won't be excited about them."

"This happened to one of my students," Jon said. "His parents pushed him to apply to eight Reach Schools. When I objected, they eventually agreed to add two Safety Schools. When this very bright kid only got into his two Safety Schools, his mom told me how sad everyone in the family was. Shoot, I was sad, too. When parents don't adjust their expectations to match reality, disappointment follows."

"The tricky part is that you can always justify adding Reach Schools by saying, 'I love you and I want you to have all the opportunities out there,'" Victoria said. "But the best way to increase Jack's opportunities is to make sure he gets into several schools that suit his personality and interests! That doesn't happen when parents tell their kids that they are 'too good' for Target or Safety Schools."

"Parents have to remind students that though college affects the future, it doesn't determine it completely," Jon said. "A student who knows what career she wants to pursue, or who is at least willing to take advantage of the opportunities presented, can flourish anywhere."

"For you and Jack, there's still plenty of time to discuss all this," Phil said. "If you realize the importance of Target and Safety Schools now, great. When it's spring of senior year and there are only two acceptances because you insisted that Jack apply to too many Reach Schools, it will be too late."

"I'm not disagreeing with you," Michelle said. "The problem is that there are so many schools out there. I don't even know how to figure out which ones might be good for Jack, especially when we're talking about Target and Safety Schools."

"That's totally normal," Victoria said. "That's also why it's so important to be open-minded about the schools you consider. If prestige is your only criterion for judging a school, then you're limited to the Top 25 Schools, but those are all Reach Schools. You have to look at factors beyond prestige."

"Like what?" Michelle asked.

"Come on, there's something I want to show you," Victoria said, jogging ahead of the group to the next landing.

Fit Factors

"What is it?" Michelle asked.

"You're going to love this," Phil said. "Everyone does."

"See for yourself," Jon said to Michelle as she climbed onto the next landing. The landing had been overrun with puppies, who were running and rolling around with great energy.

"Puppies! Can I play with them?" she asked Victoria.

"Of course!" Victoria said. "You've earned a break, and it's always good to take a minute to remind ourselves of the joy our kids feel when they attend a college that's right for them."

Michelle knelt down on the landing, and a small Boston Terrier puppy ran over to her. "There's a tag on its neck," Michelle said, grabbing it with her fingers so she could hold it still and read it. "Let's see, what's your name? Size. Size? That's kind of a strange name for a dog, isn't it?"

"These aren't your ordinary puppies," Victoria said. "These puppies are here to teach parents about Fit Factors."

"Fit Factors?" Michelle asked.

"I mean all the factors beyond prestige that families might consider when building out their College Lists, especially when it comes to those Target and Safety Schools," Victoria said.

"The Boss had us conduct a study on this, and she found that puppies were 157 percent more effective than lectures at teaching parents about Fit Factors," Jon said.

"Not a huge surprise," Phil said as he reached down to pick up another puppy that had wandered over. "This one is Setting. Want to hold her?" Phil asked Michelle.

"Of course!" Michelle said, taking hold of Setting and cradling her in her arms. "How many puppies are there?"

"Seven at the moment," Victoria said, "and they're the stars of the Stairway."

"Seven?" Michelle asked.

"Size you know," Victoria said. "For some students, whether a school is large, medium, or small is a big deal."

"And you've met Setting," Jon said. "This factor comes into play when a student has strong preferences about living in an urban, suburban, or rural area."

"This one's Academic Offerings," Phil said as a Dalmatian puppy ran over and placed his front paws on his legs. "For a student who knows what he wants to study, that means the college offers a solid program in that area. For example, a student who knows he wants to study business will want to make sure the colleges on his list offer business majors, not just economics majors."

"But Jack doesn't know what he wants to study," Michelle said. "I've been telling him for years that he's got to figure this out!"

"That's OK! I changed my major seven times," Victoria said. "You'll just want to look at schools that aren't too specialized so Jack can explore his options. This could mean a large public university with an amazing diversity of majors or a small liberal arts school with a core curriculum that will expose him to every foundational field. Just keep an open mind."

"You can also consider Academic Climate," Jon said, pointing to a fat, wrinkled puppy that wouldn't stop licking its nose. "Thinking about the level of competition versus collaboration, or how 'Type A' or 'Type B' Jack is, can prevent him from wilting in the wrong environment."

"Take the University of Chicago, for example," Victoria said. "Their unofficial motto is 'Where fun comes to die.' UChicago is a great school for some students, but not for a kid who doesn't thrive in an intense environment."

"School Culture is another Fit Factor," Phil said as a fluffy white puppy wandered aimlessly by. "If a student worked for a Republican US Congressman last summer and attends an evangelical church, she might feel out of place at a liberal college where very few classmates share her views."

"Feeling a little out of place is fine, and normal," Victoria said. "That's part of growing up. But when the feeling of alienation is too severe, it starts to interfere with the student's ability to succeed."

"Geography is another one," Jon said, pointing to a husky puppy with one blue eye and one green eye. "Not just because it affects the weather, but because it affects the opportunities available to students, like internships."

"Size, Setting, Academic Offerings, Academic Climate, School Culture, and Geography," Michelle said. "That's only six. What's the seventh?"

"Oh, right," Victoria said. "We totally forgot about Missy." A mixed-breed puppy bounded over toward the group. "'Missy' is short for 'Miscellaneous.' If the other Fit Factors don't quite cover everything for Jack, there's always Missy. She could be anything else Jack thinks his future college must have."

"Seven is still a lot to choose from," Michelle said. "Do I have to rank all of these puppies or something like that?"

"Well, once you're off this Stairway and back home with Jack, the two of you will talk it over and decide which ones you like," Victoria said. "Don't worry about how you'll know. You'll know."

"Sorry, that's a little too touchy-feely for me," Michelle said. "I want to make a rational decision."

"There's a lot of subjectivity in this process," Jon said. "Sure, there's the objective part of looking at SAT or ACT scores so you can correctly label a college as a Reach, Target, or Safety School. But once you label a school, you'll find there are dozens of schools in each category that might be good fits for Jack. At that point, how do you distinguish them? It all depends on what matters to you and Jack and on what your family is willing to pay for. That's subjective."

"Go play with the puppies already!" Phil said. "Have some fun. It's OK to be a little excited. Think about how happy Jack will be once he starts at a college that's a good fit for him!"

Needing no further encouragement, Michelle hustled off to frolic with the puppies. After a few minutes, it was clear that Setting and Geography were her favorites.

"I found two I like!" she called over. "Is that enough?"

"That's great!" Victoria called back. "Two or three is about right. Any more than that and you'll get frustrated you can't find enough colleges that match your criteria."

"Wait a second," Michelle said as she crouched down to wrestle with Setting. "What about prestige? Isn't that a Fit Factor?"

Prestige

"Not exactly," Jon said. "Don't get me wrong. Prestige matters to many families, and we'd be lying if we told you it didn't affect our own decisions. But we don't count prestige as a Fit Factor."

"The reason is prestige is the same as selectivity," Phil said. "The lower a school's acceptance rate is, the more prestigious it is usually perceived to be. But we already deal with selectivity when categorizing a college as a Reach, Target, or Safety School. There's no need to double count it by making it a Fit Factor, too."

"Think of it this way," Jon said. "If you chose schools only based on prestige, you'd end up with a list full of Reach Schools. So you need other Fit Factors to be able to choose Target and Safety Schools."

"Also, there are huge differences even among prestigious schools," Victoria said. "Take Brown and Cornell. Both are Ivy League schools that would be Reach Schools for Jack, but that doesn't mean they're interchangeable. Brown is somewhat urban. It's located in Providence, Rhode Island, which is a vibrant, medium-sized city, and it attracts students who are socially and politically motivated to do good in the world. Cornell is located in a fun college town surrounded by gorgeous nature, and it attracts students who are a bit more focused on the practical or pre-professional applications of their knowledge."

"That's why regardless of how prestigious a school might be, you still have to keep an open mind about whether it's a good fit for Jack," Jon said.

"Keeping an open mind can be even harder when it comes to adding Target and Safety Schools to the College List," Phil said. "Lots of parents look at the schools I suggest for these categories and say those schools aren't good enough for their child."

"Or say that their child is too smart for those schools," Jon said.

"Or say they would never pay for that school," Victoria said.

"But it's impossible to put together a list that has Target and Safety Schools without having an open mind," Jon said.

"Quality does matter, though," Michelle said. "Doesn't it make sense to say I'd pay more for Harvard than for some private college I've never heard of?"

"Sure, but that's not really the issue," Jon said. "After all, Harvard is a Reach School for everyone, and we're talking about how to find Target and Safety Schools."

"Not to mention the fact that just because you haven't heard of it doesn't mean it's bad," Victoria said. "Many families have never heard of Babson, but for a kid who is dead set on becoming an entrepreneur, it's a great choice."

"Plus there are plenty of great Target and Safety School options that can end up being just as affordable as in-state public schools," Phil said.

"How?" Michelle asked. "I don't know where I'm supposed to find all these affordable Target and Safety Schools."

"Public Honors Colleges and Honors Programs," Jon said. "These offer benefits such as scholarships, smaller classes, honors classes, and extra opportunities for internships and research. The perks vary from school to school, but John Willingham's Public University Honors website and his *Inside Honors* book are great resources on the topic."

"For starters, you can check out the Honors Colleges at schools like Arizona State, Clemson, Maryland, Oregon, Penn State, South Carolina, and Ohio University," Phil said.

"Arizona State?" Michelle asked, raising her eyebrows. "Jack needs to be around other smart kids."

"Why is everyone so negative about Arizona State?" Jon asked. "I even had an ASU alum give me exactly the same response! What you might not know is that Barrett Honors College at Arizona State is the premier Honors College in the country."

"Open mind, remember?" Phil asked Michelle.

"OK, OK, I can't promise Jack will apply there, but we'll at least take a look," Michelle said.

"That's all we're asking," Victoria said.

"What about private schools?" Michelle asked. "I still don't want to pay $70,000 per year for some no-name school."

Victoria glanced at Jon and Phil, who both nodded. "We'd better talk about financial aid," Victoria said.

Financial Aid

"First off, the $70,000 number you hear about is the sticker price, not the actual price that most students pay," Jon said.

"Kind of like retail price versus wholesale price?" Michelle asked.

"Exactly," Phil said. "Most families don't end up paying retail. To get an estimate of what you'd actually pay, google 'Net Price Calculator' and the name of the college."

"Don't put this off too long," Victoria said. "When cost is an issue — which is most of the time — you need to make sure some of those Target and Safety Schools are within your family's budget. That way, where Jack gets accepted matches up with what you can afford."

"There's nothing worse than realizing for the first time in spring of senior year, after one of your kid's favorite schools has already accepted him, that it's not affordable," Jon said. "Sure, after looking at the Net Price Calculators and discussing with Jack, you still might decide he should apply to some schools that look too expensive. Maybe the financial aid package will be more generous than expected. But at least you do that with eyes wide open, and Jack knows ahead of time you might not be able to afford it."

"You should look into need-based financial aid, too," Phil said, "but you have to apply for it."

"I know, I know," Michelle said. "My friend Jennifer has a son who is a senior, and she started to explain it to me, but my eyes just glazed over. I've been putting it off. It seems so complicated."

Draggin roared out from below. As Michelle and the three College Fates looked down the Stairway, they saw Draggin exhale a 25-foot streak of flame in their direction.

"We're not financial aid experts, but we want you to know the basics," Victoria said. "That starts with understanding where financial aid comes from."

"That's great," Michelle said. "I wouldn't mind finding Jack some scholarships."

"Financial aid isn't just scholarships, also known as grants or free money," Jon said. "It includes loans, even though those have to paid back. It also includes work-study, which is a part-time job that allows a student to earn money to pay for college."

"Seriously?" Michelle said. "You're telling me that loans and part-time jobs are financial aid?"

"I'm afraid so," Victoria said. "When colleges say 'financial aid,' they're talking about scholarships, loans, and work-study. You can't look only at the amount of the financial aid package. You have to pay attention to the type of financial aid you're getting, too."

"But you said I have to apply for financial aid," Michelle said. "So how does it work?"

"That depends on where the financial aid comes from," Jon said. "Most financial aid comes from one of two sources," Jon said. "The first source is the federal government. That's Federal Financial Aid, which is all need-based. The second source is the colleges. That's Institutional Financial Aid, which can be need-based or merit-based."

"To apply for Federal Financial Aid such as grants, loans, and work-study, Jack will need to complete and submit the Free Application for Federal Student Aid, more commonly known as the FAFSA," Phil said.

"You can get an estimate of the Federal Financial Aid Jack qualifies for by googling the Department of Education's FAFSA4caster tool," Victoria said.

"To apply for Institutional Financial Aid at many colleges, Jack will need to complete and submit a form called the CSS Profile," Phil said. "It's a form administered by the College Board, the same folks who bring you the SAT."

"How do I know which schools require the FAFSA and which require the CSS Profile?" Michelle asked.

"Check each college's financial aid website," Victoria said. "These financial aid applications should be done by fall of senior year, and be forewarned — it's annoying, like doing your taxes — so start early! Especially when it comes to the CSS Profile, which is extremely detailed compared to the FAFSA."

"How do the FAFSA and CSS Profile formulas work, though?" Michelle asked. "My friend Jennifer I was telling you about went to some free seminar where an insurance guy said it's possible to move some assets around to increase financial aid."

"The FAFSA and the CSS Profile are based on the same idea," Jon said. "They look at student income, student assets, parent income, and parent assets, and they 'tax' each at a different rate to determine the Expected Family Contribution, or EFC, which is the amount the college believes the family can afford to pay."

"In simplest terms, the FAFSA and CSS Profile differ in that they allow different 'deductions' — for example, the FAFSA excludes your primary residence as a parent asset while the CSS Profile does not," Victoria said. "Also, the two forms apply different 'tax rates' to different sources of funds."

"Which is why the Expected Family Contribution is one number for a college using the FAFSA and another number, often a higher number, for a college using the CSS Profile," Phil said.

"I have a practical question," Michelle said. "Will applying for financial aid hurt Jack's chances?"

"If you know you need financial aid or just aren't sure, you should apply for it," Jon said. "If you're fortunate enough to be 100 percent sure you won't need financial aid, then don't apply. Not applying will give Jack an admissions advantage at need-aware schools."

"Need-aware?" Michelle asked.

"That means the student's ability to pay is an admissions factor," Victoria said. "Some schools are need-blind, meaning they don't care about your ability to pay, but many don't have that luxury."

"Not applying for financial aid isn't an option for us," Michelle said. "Is there any way I can increase his chances for financial aid?"

"Because college is so expensive, there are always people out there making presentations about how to increase financial aid, like the insurance agent your friend Jennifer told you about," Jon said. "The pitch is pretty straightforward. Basically, move assets or income into a category that the financial aid form excludes or that it 'taxes' at a lower rate. That will decrease your Expected Family Contribution and increase your financial aid award, the thinking goes."

"Does it work?" Michelle asked.

"I'm skeptical of anyone proposing a simple solution to a complex problem," Jon said. "Many of these asset-shifting solutions are being peddled by insurance agents who are more focused on the hefty fees they'll earn from selling a whole life policy than by what's best for the family's overall financial health. I've seen cases where the proposed solution lowers the Expected Family Contribution for the FAFSA calculation but not for the CSS Profile calculation. That should increase financial aid from colleges that only require the FAFSA, but it won't increase financial aid from colleges that also require the CSS Profile. Even if some magical financial product increases your financial aid, you still have to compare the cost of that product with the amount and type of the financial aid you're likely to receive. Be skeptical, and ask questions!"

"There are plenty of great people out there who provide more detailed information about financial aid," Phil said. "Take a look at what Mark Kantrowitz says on his FinAid website and at what Lynn O'Shaughnessy says in her *The College Solution* book and website."

"If you're still not sure what's what, seek out an independent financial advisor who is familiar with the FAFSA and the CSS Profile."

"I'll take a look," Michelle said, "but to be honest, I don't think we're going to qualify for need-based aid."

"That's where Merit Aid comes in," Victoria said. "Students with strong GPAs and SAT scores can find plenty of free money if they look outside the Top 25 Schools."

"You'll take a hit on prestige, but if Merit Aid makes a private school cost the same as an in-state public school, sometimes the private school fits the student's needs better," Phil said.

"Let me give you an example," Jon said. "I had a California student who got so much Merit Aid at Santa Clara University, a private school, that it was actually cheaper than going to UC Berkeley, a public school. Once Merit Aid took affordability out of the discussion, the family could focus on which school was a better fit for the student."

"No one is saying that Jack getting into a Safety School will be as exciting as him getting into a Reach School," Victoria said. "We're saying since your list needs Target and Safety Schools anyway, you might as well find the best possible Target and Safety Schools for Jack. Sometimes best means most affordable."

"That's why public Honors Colleges and private colleges with Merit Aid are such an important part of building the College List," Phil said.

"Can I figure out exactly how much Merit Aid Jack will get?" Michelle asked.

"Sometimes the websites will have a Merit Aid calculator," Jon said. "God bless Baylor for showing you exactly how much higher your SAT score needs to be to qualify for more aid. Sometimes you can find Merit Aid in the Net Price Calculator. If the info isn't on the website, you can call the school's financial aid office or talk to parents of students who have gone through the process recently."

"If Jack's PSAT score ends up high enough for him to become a National Merit Finalist, you should spend some time researching which schools offer him Merit Aid for that," Victoria said. "Jack might qualify for half-tuition at the University of Southern California or full tuition plus stipends and housing benefits at the University of Alabama, just to name a couple."

How to Find Good Fit Colleges

"That's good to know," Michelle said. "I get that I need to be open-minded about where Jack applies, and that Jack needs affordable Target and Safety Schools that match his Fit Factors. But practically speaking, where do I find the names of these colleges?"

"The easiest way is *The Fiske Guide to Colleges*," Jon said. "It gives detailed written summaries of more than 300 colleges. That's really helpful in differentiating schools when you're in the early stages of building a list and need to know the feel of the school."

"Beyond *Fiske*, there's always *Colleges That Change Lives*," Victoria said. "The *Colleges That Change Lives* book and website highlight a group of about 40 schools that focus on cultivating a love of learning. That's your best bet for finding a hidden gem."

"There's also the college search feature at the College Board's Big Future website," Phil said. "If you enter Jack's Fit Factors, you'll get dozens of results, some of which you've probably never heard of."

"Whether you use *Fiske*, *Colleges That Change Lives*, or Big Future isn't as important as the mindset you bring," Jon said.

"I know, keep an open mind, I heard you," Michelle said.

"Once you or Jack finds a school that looks interesting, you can check out the college's own website," Jon said. "So start with the general overviews from *Fiske*, *Colleges That Change Lives*, and Big Future, and then work toward the detailed info on the college websites. It takes time, but it's not complicated. You'll figure it out."

The group came to a halt in front of a sign welded to the railing. "College Heaven: 6,524 steps."

Words of Wisdom from the Boss

"A good College List maximizes the quantity and quality of choices your child has for college. Part of building the list is objective: correctly labeling each college as a Reach, Target, or Safety School and then ensuring the list contains a mix of three Reach, four Target, and three Safety Schools. Part of building the list is subjective: discussing and deciding as a family which Fit Factors matter to you. Common Fit Factors include size, setting, academic offerings, academic climate, school culture, and geography. You have to look beyond prestige, or else your child's list won't have enough Target and Safety Schools."

"Do you know what scares me most about Jack applying to college?" Michelle asked. The three College Fates paused and waited. "It's like that feeling I have on the way to the airport before a big trip. I think I've packed everything, but I keep asking myself, 'Did I turn off the stove? Did I bring my sunglasses? Did I lock the front door?' In all the rush to get somewhere, there's this nagging feeling that I missed something."

"That's normal," Jon said. "College planning takes years, and there's a lot to get done, especially from spring of junior year through fall of senior year."

"Most of it is what you'd expect," Phil said. "You know grades are important, and so is taking challenging classes. We talked about the SAT, ACT, and Test Prep. And we've covered the basics of how to put together a good College List."

"There's the application itself, and the application essays," Victoria said. "We'll cover those in a little bit."

"What am I missing, then?" Michelle asked.

"If I had to guess, I would say Demonstrated Interest," Victoria said.

"That's a general term for actions a student takes to show interest in a college," Phil said.

"Colleges care about that?" Michelle said.

"Yes, many colleges consider Demonstrated Interest in the admissions process," Victoria said, "though some don't. Chances are, at least some of the schools on Jack's College List will be keeping an eye on it."

"How do I know which ones care and which ones don't?" Michelle asked.

"The Common Data Set," Jon said. "It's a standardized survey many colleges complete every year, and it's full of useful statistics."

"Many parents are surprised to learn that the Common Data Set includes info about how colleges make their admissions decisions," Phil said. "Section C7 in a school's Common Data Set response covers which academic and nonacademic admissions factors are 'very important,' 'important,' 'considered,' or 'not considered.'"

"To figure out what role Demonstrated Interest plays for a particular college, you'll want to pay attention to the admission factors in Section C7 that are labeled 'Interview' and 'Applicant's Level of Interest,'" Jon said. "Those are your main clues."

"To find the Common Data Set for a school, just google 'Common Data Set' and the name of the college," Phil said. "For example, 'Common Data Set University of Minnesota.'"

Draggin let forth another loud roar from below. "Let's keep moving," Phil said. He increased his pace from a walk to a slow jog.

"Phil's right!" Jon said. "We should pick up the pace."

"When it comes to demonstrating interest, you have to be bold!" Victoria added. "One of my students was on campus for a summer program, and she decided she wanted to meet President Faust of Harvard University. After wandering across Harvard Yard, she went into the building, walked straight past the administrative assistant, and into the Office of the President. While President Faust was understandably surprised by my student's visit, she introduced herself, they started chatting, and my student successfully arranged a presidential interview for admission."

"You're joking, right?" Michelle said.

"No, it's true," Victoria said. "She didn't apply in the end, but I admire her boldness. Jack might not be that bold, and most 17-year-olds aren't, either. But the bolder Jack can be, the better."

"I like the idea of demonstrating interest," Michelle said. "I just don't know how to go about it."

"That's what we'll show you as we walk up the Rainbow Road," Jon said.

"Rainbow Road?" Michelle asked.

"What can I say?" Victoria said. "The Boss loves rainbows and musical numbers. This section of the Stairway was inspired by Judy Garland's performance of 'Over the Rainbow.'"

"The journey to College Heaven starts with the dreams parents dare to dream for their children," Phil said. "Then it continues with the dreams that children dare to dream for themselves."

"It will make more sense once you see it for yourself," Jon said. "Let's go!"

Responding to Marketing Materials

The group trotted up the Stairway until they reached a step completely blocked by an ivy-covered brick wall, which contained an arched wooden door painted red. Michelle pushed it, but it wouldn't open. She looked over at the three College Fates.

"Over there, in the ivy to the right," Phil said.

Michelle turned to the right and moved her hands under the ivy. "There's something here," Michelle said, bringing her hands to a stop.

"What's inside?" Victoria asked.

"I'm not sure," Michelle said, pulling back the ivy and revealing a small plastic box full of brochures and a sign that read, "Please take one." "Marketing materials, really?" Michelle flipped open the lid of the box and removed a brochure. "HEAVENLY U," the top line read. To the right of the top line was the Heavenly U logo, which consisted of a halo over the top of a letter H. Below that was a picture of smiling, ethnically diverse students kissed by rays of sunshine as they strolled across a campus quad strewn with autumn leaves. Below the picture was a slogan: "Collaboration. Community. Calling." "I'm not sure those are the words that will set many teenage hearts racing with desire. What am I supposed to do with this brochure, anyway?" Michelle uncovered the plastic box in the ivy-covered wall again, opened the lid, and started to place her brochure at the top of the stack inside.

"Wait!" Victoria said, grabbing Michelle's arm. "I know these brochures all look the same after a while. But no, you can't just put it back."

"Look at the back page," Phil said. Michelle unfolded the brochure and flipped it over. The last page contained a tear-away postcard with instructions to return for more information.

"We get these brochures all the time," Michelle said. "I've been piling them up in a stack on my counter."

From far below, Draggin let out a roar. Michelle and the three College Fates turned their heads toward the bottom of the Stairway just in time to see Draggin exhale a giant fireball up the Stairway. It soared right toward them, clearing the brick wall with just inches to spare.

"Stop procrastinating with those marketing materials!" Jon said to Michelle. "Those aren't just for looking at. You have to take action! Tell Jack to fill those out and send them back in."

"OK, OK!" Michelle said. "I'll make sure he fills out requests from colleges for contact information. If those schools care enough to invite him to apply, then the least he can do is show some interest, right?"

"Whoa, wait, what did you say?" Victoria asked. "Don't get me wrong, Jack should respond to marketing materials. But don't read too much into the fact that he's getting these brochures in the mail."

"It's marketing," Jon said. "Colleges have limited budgets, so they buy student names from organizations like the College Board. They're doing what they can to get students to apply."

"So respond to marketing materials, but don't read too much into them," Michelle said. "Got it."

As Michelle spoke, the red door swung open, revealing a flight of red steps on the other side.

Signing Up for Email Lists

One by one, the members of the group walked through the doorway. They walked up the steps until they reached another ivy-covered brick wall, this one with an orange door. An iPad was embedded in the wall to the right of the door. The Heavenly U logo occupied the middle of the screen. Below the logo, there was a button that read, "Touch me."

"Wow, these schools aren't shy about asking for affection," Michelle said.

"It can seem a bit desperate," Victoria said, "but it comes from a good place. What happens if you touch the screen?"

Michelle tapped the button, and the screen changed. "Join our email list!" the screen read, as the sounds of soothing harp music poured forth from the iPad's speakers.

"An email list?" Michelle asked. "Do I have to? No, it's fine. I can use my throwaway email."

"No!" Phil said. "Don't use your email address. Colleges don't care about *your* interest! Well except for your interest in paying tuition. They want to know *Jack's* interest."

"Use Jack's email address, not yours," Jon said. "Make sure it's professional, like one that includes his first and last name, not 'surfbro7' or whatever account he made when he was in fourth grade. That way, when he uses that same email address for his college applications, the school will make the connection."

"Can't we do this later?" Michelle asked. Draggin let out another loud roar.

"You already know the answer," Victoria said. "Sign Jack up now and get it over with!"

"That's annoying," Michelle said. "Do I have to do this for every school?"

"We're having you do this one so you know what to tell Jack," Victoria said. "Jack should do it himself for all the schools that consider Demonstrated Interest. Just because it's annoying doesn't mean he can skip it."

"Make sure Jack is checking his email, too," Jon said. "You have to make sure emails from colleges go to his inbox and not to spam. And remind him to click on the links in any emails he gets from colleges."

"That really matters?" Michelle asked.

"Suppose you were an admissions officer deciding between two applicants with equally strong grades, SAT scores, Letters of Recommendation, and extracurriculars," Phil said. "If one of those applicants never opened your emails while the other one opened every email and clicked on all the links, which one would you want?" Phil said.

"Point taken," Michelle said as she tapped at the iPad to enter Jack's email. "There, done," she said, giving the iPad one more tap. "He is signed up for the email list."

With that announcement, the orange door swung open, revealing a flight of orange steps above. The group filed through the doorway and continued its climb.

Following Colleges on Social Media

Soon enough, Michelle and the three College Fates arrived at another brick wall, this one with a bright yellow door. Mounted on the door were placards showing the logos of all the major social media sites. The blue Twitter bird, the Snapchat ghost, the Instagram camera, and even the much maligned Facebook "f" were all there.

"What are those for?" Michelle said.

"Do you still have your phone?" Victoria asked.

"I'm not sure I get service," Michelle said, pulling her iPhone from her pocket. "Ooh, just kidding, yes I do. But why?"

"Time for Jack's social media check-up," Phil said. "Let's see what kind of online presence he has. Can you show me his Twitter feed?"

Everyone crowded around Michelle to see. A few taps later and the group was treated to a picture of several smiling high school boys and girls holding half-filled margarita glasses. "Looks like Jack and his friends really enjoyed themselves when you were out of town last weekend," Jon said.

"That's so awesome you have a hot tub in your backyard!" Victoria said.

"Girls' Weekend," Michelle said. "It's a once-a-year thing. I told Jack, 'No parties!' and he promised me he was studying! Just wait until I talk to that boy."

"Let's take a look at Facebook," Jon said. Michelle tapped away.

"Nothing," Phil said. "Just the profile pic."

"What about Instagram and Snapchat?" Victoria asked. Michelle tapped away at her screen again.

"Nothing there, either," Phil said. "It looks like Jack has adjusted the privacy settings, so that's good. It's just Twitter that's a problem."

"I've seen everything from curse words to breasts on my students' social media accounts," Victoria said.

"Don't even get me started on the eggplant emojis," Jon said.

"We just don't need colleges seeing this sort of thing," Phil said.

"Or employers!" Michelle said. "Can you imagine what will happen if Jack is interviewing for a job somewhere and his Twitter account looks like this?"

"Keep the publicly accessible stuff G-rated, or just don't post publicly at all," Victoria said. "The really proactive students can use social media to showcase their talents and interests. But let's be honest, for most students, it's more a matter of cleaning up questionable material or at least fixing the privacy settings."

"Once Jack cleans up his accounts, he can start using them to interact with colleges," Phil said.

"Following them on Facebook, for example," Jon said. "But it's more than just following and liking. This is an easy way for Jack to ask questions and get to know the colleges."

"But I can't fix all his accounts now," Michelle said. "How will we get through this door?"

"Text Jack," Phil said. "Ask him to change the privacy settings on his Twitter account."

"OK," Michelle said. She tapped out three texts in quick succession. Her phone vibrated almost immediately. "Three embarrassed face emoji. 'Sorry mom, fixing it rn,' he says. Oh, good."

As Michelle finished speaking, the yellow door opened, and the group walked through it to a flight of yellow stairs.

Cultivating Relationships with Admissions Reps

They could see another brick wall up ahead, this one with a green door, flung wide open. The group passed through and continued climbing, the green steps growing wider and wider.

"Why are these steps so wide?" Michelle asked. "And what are all those people doing up there?" On each of the remaining steps was a table. Draped over each table was a banner with the name and logo of a college. On top of each table lay glossy color brochures and tchotchkes. Branded pens, flash drives, and stress balls all vied for the attention of passersby. "What is this place? There must be over 100 tables!"

"This is a zoo," Jon said. "Also known as a College Fair."

"Will Princeton be here?" Michelle asked, straining her neck to catch a glimpse of the names on the banners hanging from the tables. "What about MIT?"

"Well… the Stairway's College Fair is a bit different," Jon said. "It's all schools that haven't been founded yet. The Boss saw this as win-win-win. The parents on the Stairway get some ideas about how to coach their kids. The not-yet-born colleges get real-time, face-to-face feedback from their target customers about their offerings. The Boss collects a nice little Stairway access fee from the colleges, and that money gets reinvested into Stairway repairs, like for all the sections of iron railing that keep getting melted by Draggin's fireballs."

"College Fairs are overcrowded and overwhelming, but Jack can use them to meet the representatives from the colleges he's interested in," Victoria said. "We're doing a practice run with you here to make sure you know how to prep him."

"Jack's not there just to collect pamphlets and keychains," Phil said. "He has to make an impression."

"Often the reps at these College Fairs are the same ones who will do the first read of students' applications," Jon said.

"How should he open the conversation with these admissions reps?" Michelle asked.

"I tell my students to start with their name and then to add an interesting piece of personal information," Victoria said.

"Finishing with a question doesn't hurt, either," Phil said. "Especially if it's a question that shows interest in the school."

"So Jack can introduce himself with his name, an interesting fact about himself, and a question about the college," Michelle said.

"You got it," Victoria said. "For example, I'd say, 'Hi! My name is Victoria and I've been to see Michelangelo's Sistine Chapel ceiling over 200 times. I've heard such great things about your school's art history program, but could you tell me a little more about it?'"

"And I would say something like, 'My name is Phil, and I'm the sports editor for the school paper, *The Accolade*. I'm interested in your school's journalism and English departments. Are they popular majors?' Now you," Phil prompted Michelle.

"Hmm…" Michelle said. "Let me think." She drummed her fingers on the rail of the Stairway and looked out into the distance. "I'd say, 'My name is Michelle, and I've been a foster parent to five children. I'm interested in learning more about developmental psychology. What can you tell me about your program?'"

"That's perfect!" Jon said. "Why don't you practice introducing yourself at those tables? Then you'll be ready to help Jack when the time comes." Jon motioned toward the tables on the green steps stretching from where they stood up to the blue door. "We'll meet you at the blue door in a little bit."

The three College Fates continued up the green stairs, leaving Michelle on her own to introduce herself to the admissions reps. When they all met up 20 minutes later, Michelle was carrying a tote bag full of brochures and swag. "That was awesome! I was a little nervous for the first few, but then it got easier. I didn't realize how much the psychology programs vary from school to school. And the rep from Nevaeh College gave me her card and told me to reach out to her with any questions. I never would have thought about Jack applying to a school like Nevaeh, but this fair changed my perspective!"

"That's exactly the College Fair experience we want Jack to have," Phil said. "All it takes is a little preparation."

"And a little follow-up," Jon said. Michelle and the three College Fates walked past the final table, waved at the Zenith University rep, and sat down in front of the next door in the Stairway, which was painted royal blue. "You're not done with the College Fair until you've sent out thank-you emails. Why don't you take a few minutes to sort through all the pamphlets and jot down some notes on your five favorite colleges from today?"

"You can include any questions you didn't get answered, since those will make for great material for your thank-you emails," Phil said.

"Even if Jack never attends a College Fair, he can still get to know admission reps," Victoria said. "It can be as simple as attending an info session when a rep visits Jack's high school. I also have my students email admissions reps to ask questions at least once in the process."

"If Jack's going to be sending emails to admissions reps, maybe I should proofread them," Michelle said.

"Not a bad idea," Jon said. "We want them to sound professional. That means proper punctuation and spelling, and also addressing the admissions rep as 'Mr.' or 'Ms.' rather than using the indeterminate but ever-popular 'Hey!' which I still delight in seeing from time to time."

"And remind Jack to actually say, 'Thank you!'" Victoria said. "Whether Jack meets an admissions rep during a college visit, a College Fair, a high school presentation, or anywhere else, a thank-you is always welcome."

"Can you give me a minute to write out my notes?" Michelle asked, pulling a Nevaeh College pen and notepad from her tote bag and sitting down on the step nearest the blue door.

"No problem," Jon said. The three College Fates meandered over to chat with the Zenith University rep as Michelle scribbled away.

"OK, done!" Michelle called out a couple minutes later. "I know exactly what I need to do to prepare Jack to get to know admissions reps."

The blue door swung open, revealing a flight of blue steps.

Visiting Colleges

"The blue steps are the college visit section of the Rainbow Road," Victoria told Michelle as they walked through the blue door.

"Is a college visit really necessary?" Michelle said. "Jack's schedule is packed, and I have work. Not to mention it would be expensive to visit ten colleges, especially when we don't even know if Jack will get in!"

"I wouldn't say necessary," Victoria said, "but chances are that you'll go on at least a few. And if Jack is applying to local schools that care about Demonstrated Interest, a visit is one of the best ways to do that."

"You don't have to fly across the country just to visit a school, but if the school is close by, the way University of San Diego is for Southern California kids or Santa Clara University is for Northern California kids, then it's practically a must," Jon said.

"Visits are for determining fit, too, not just for demonstrating interest," Phil said. "Even if the school doesn't track Demonstrated Interest, or even if Jack visits a school and hates it, he's still making progress in figuring out what kind of school he's looking for."

"An easy way for Jack to learn more about his preferences is to visit a large, medium, and small college in your area," Victoria said. "Whether or not he's seriously considering any of them, visiting will give him a good feel for what size school he wants."

"It's not a real college visit without a tour," Jon said. "Our guides should be here any minute."

"There they are!" Phil said, waving at two figures jogging down the stairs toward Michelle and the three College Fates. "Right on time." The two guides wore matching khaki shorts, periwinkle blue polo shirts with Heavenly U logos embroidered in white, and flip flops.

"Hey, I'm Barbie! What's up?" the first chirped as she approached Michelle.

"And I'm Ken!" the second one said.

"Ken and Barbie?" Michelle asked, turning to Jon.

"The Boss now requires all guides working the Stairway to be bubbly and non-threatening," Jon said. "No need to make applying to college more intimidating than it already is."

"Are you ready to start your college tour?" Barbie asked. "We're so excited you decided to come visit!"

"I never thought I'd see you and Ken leading a college tour," Michelle said. "Shouldn't you be in Malibu?"

"That place is so, like, superficial," Barbie said.

"Totally surface level, dude," Ken said. "We really wanted a deeper experience, so that's why we work up here on the Stairway. Being up here, far from the madding crowd, is just totally fulfilling, you know what I mean? But let's talk about you and your son, yeah? What brings you here? Did you sign up for a tour?"

Michelle looked over at the three College Fates.

"We reserved a space for her through the Heavenly U website," Victoria said.

"Great! I'm so glad you did!" Barbie said. "Sometimes we have families just wandering across campus looking at the buildings. But when they haven't signed up for the tour and info session, we have no idea who they are."

"You have to sign up for tours in advance to make sure the college tracks Jack's visit," Phil said to Michelle. "And sometimes tours are full and won't accept walk-ins."

"Well, shall we get started?" Barbie said, beginning to walk backward up the Stairway.

"Wait! Look out!" Michelle called out. Yet just as Barbie's heel was about to clip the next step and send her toppling over backwards, she lifted her foot barely enough to be able to set it down on the next step.

"Don't worry," Ken said. "We train for hours to be able to walk backward. It's like instinct for us now."

"No matter how many times I climb this Stairway, it still impresses me," Jon said.

"Aw, thanks, dude!" Ken said. "Right on. Well, so let me tell you about today's tour. Actually since the Stairway won't be a part of the Heavenly U campus, this will be more like an info session."

"You'll learn all about the school," Barbie chimed in, "and we'll give you some tips about the application essays. But we won't go into too much detail about the essays because the three College Fates will cover that later, right, guys?" Barbie paused to look over at the three College Fates, and Jon gave a thumbs-up. "Perfect."

"Are most college visits just tours and info sessions?" Michelle asked the three College Fates.

"Pretty much," Victoria said. "But with some planning, they can be more than that. Before you and Jack visit, ask him to email the admissions rep to let her know he'll be on campus."

"The admissions rep?" Michelle asked. "You mean the one Jack met at the College Fair?"

"Right!" Phil said. "That's the idea. And if he hasn't been to a College Fair, he can check the college's website or call the admissions office to figure out who his rep is."

"If Jack has a specific interest like — what was it you said earlier?" Victoria asked.

"I don't know," Michelle said. "Maybe computer science, maybe business."

"Either one works," Victoria said. "Then Jack can ask the admissions rep if it will be possible for him to sit in on a computer science or business course. That's a chance for him to get a feel for one of the professors and to see if he fits in with the other students."

"That feeling of 'I could see myself here' is one of the mysterious parts of the application process," Jon said. "If Jack is choosing which of two similar Target Schools to include on his College List, that feeling from the visit can be a determining factor. One of my students knew as soon as he set foot on the Harvey Mudd campus that it wasn't right for him, and he's happy studying engineering at University of Illinois instead."

"If you do college visits with Jack, you have to remember to take some notes about your impressions about the tour, the info session, and anything else you observed or experienced while on campus," Phil said. "These notes can give an extra level of detail to any Why This College Essay Jack will probably have to write."

"Oh, and can I add something that's super-annoying on college visits?" Barbie asked. "I mean, I know you would never do this. But some parents ask all the questions and don't let their kids talk at all."

"Yeah, I totally hate that," Ken said. "The visit is about the student like bonding with the school on a deep, spiritual level, you know what I mean? All that talking from the parents just messes with the positive energy. You just have to let Jack take the lead, OK, Mom?"

"Of course!" Michelle said, smiling at Ken, and then turning to Victoria to roll her eyes.

"Should we keep going? I'd love to tell you more about Heavenly U," Barbie said. "Did you know that Heavenly U is the only college that will let its students do hands-on engineering work on a fully operational hyperloop?" She gestured to the hyperloop tube attached to the Stairway's rail. "Working on the hyperloop will give our students valuable real-world experience that will help them when they apply for jobs and internships."

"We anticipate that 106 percent of Heavenly U graduates will be fully employed within six months after graduation," Ken said.

"106 percent?" Michelle whispered to Victoria. "That doesn't even make sense!"

"Colleges and numbers," Victoria whispered back. "It gets a little weird sometimes."

"If you have any questions, feel free to stop us and let us know," Barbie said, pausing her speech to look at Michelle.

Michelle nodded and smiled. "Thank you, I will," she said.

As the party continued climbing up the blue stairs, Ken and Barbie walked backwards effortlessly, always smiling. Whenever they stopped speaking, they smiled. Speak. Smile. Speak. Smile. The presentation was a cheerfully delivered mixture of Heavenly U facts, trivia, and new traditions. The Hook Hyperloop was the brainchild of Caltech dropouts, but don't worry, college is definitely important. The Eastern Gate of the Heavenly U campus would remain locked at all times, except on graduation day, when all the new graduates would walk through it at sunrise, symbolizing their glorious entry into an otherwise dull and backward real world. And so on. For 45 minutes.

"That brings us to the end of our tour," Barbie said as the group reached the last blue stairs. Ahead they could see another brick wall, this one with an indigo door.

Jon nudged Michelle's arm gently with his elbow. "Huh, what?" she said, snapping her head in Jon's direction.

"The tour is over, so we're going to say goodbye to Barbie and Ken now," Jon said.

"Thank you so much!" Michelle said. She reached to shake hands first with Barbie and then with Ken.

"If you have any questions, feel free to get in touch with your admissions rep, Angel," Ken said. "Here's his business card." Ken offered the white business card with gold embossed print, and Michelle accepted it.

"We'll see you the day after tomorrow," Phil said. "The Boss has us upstairs all day tomorrow for a training seminar. We're getting updated on the latest and greatest field-tested techniques for handling helicopter parents, plus a quick intro to bulldozer parents, which we're told is the latest unfortunate trend in child-rearing."

"Bulldozer parents, sounds intense," Ken said. "But it's good to stay up-to-date. Well, we have to run... we have another session starting in five minutes. Nice talking to all of you today!"

"Bye, now!" Barbie said with a smile and a wave.

Ken and Barbie then jogged down the blue stairs until they disappeared from the view of Michelle and the three College Fates. "What now?" Michelle asked.

"Well, you tell us," Victoria said. "When Jack finishes a college visit, what should he do?"

"Jot down some notes," Michelle said. "And if he has questions, he can email the admissions rep."

"There's another aspect of the college visit that Ken and Barbie didn't touch on, but it's worth mentioning," Jon said.

"What's that?" Michelle asked.

"Summer programs at college campuses," Jon said. "At some schools, these serve the function of extended visits: a supercharged way to demonstrate interest in a school, especially if the student decides to apply Early Decision the following fall."

"And especially if the student can make connections with a grad student or professor at the school who ends up willing to write a Letter of Recommendation," Victoria said.

"Demonstrated Interest isn't the only reason to participate in a summer program," Phil said. "Remember fit! If an on-campus program helps Jack figure out what type of campus or which area of study suits him, that's still valuable."

"This never would have occurred to me," Michelle said.

"That's what we're here for!" Jon said as the group made its way up to the indigo door.

Applying Early Action or Early Decision

As they drew close to the indigo door, it swung open. "It's a lot of information to take in," she said, "and I don't blame you for looking a bit dazed when Barbie and Ken were talking."

"They're just so... cheerful," Michelle said. "It's exhausting."

"Fortunately, we're done with college visits for now," Phil said. "After you." Phil gestured to the open doorway. Michelle stepped through, and the three College Fates followed close behind.

"That's different," Michelle said. The next brick wall, which contained a violet door, was just ten steps above. On the landing in front of the violet door stood two tables. "What's that up there?"

"See for yourself," Jon said. The group trotted up the stairs and examined the table on the left.

"This looks like a roulette wheel," Michelle said. "So I just place a bet and see what happens?"

"Almost," Victoria said. "There are two green spaces, and you win if the ball lands on either one of them. This is Regular Decision Roulette."

"What about the other side?" Michelle asked, walking over to the table on the other side of the Stairway.

"That's Early Decision Roulette," Phil said. "Same rules as Regular Decision Roulette — green wins."

"This wheel has twice as many green spaces, though," Michelle said, pointing to the four green spaces on the wheel. "Why bother with Regular Decision Roulette? My odds are twice as good over here."

"Place your bet!" Phil said, removing a white and gold poker chip from his robe and handing it to Michelle, who immediately placed it on a green square on the Early Decision Roulette table. Phil spun the Early Decision Roulette wheel counterclockwise and then flung the small, white roulette ball clockwise. The group watched the ball bounce over the red, black, and green slots on the wheel, waiting for it to stop.

"Hey!" Michelle called out, grabbing Victoria's arm. "That's not fair!"

"What do you mean?" Victoria asked.

"There are only two green spaces now," Michelle said. "But the wheel started out with four! What's going on here?"

Michelle was right. Two of the green spaces on the Early Decision Roulette wheel had vanished.

"It took the Boss almost a year to perfect the optical illusion of the extra green spaces on this wheel," Jon said. "When you're talking to Jack about Early Decision, we want you to remember that the odds aren't always as good as they first appear."

The bouncing ball came to rest in a red slot. "Maybe next time," Phil said.

"The idea behind applying Early Decision is that the student applies by an earlier deadline — typically November 1st instead of January 1st — and receives an admissions decision by an earlier date — typically December 15th instead of April 1st," Jon said. "Early Decision is binding, so each student can only apply to one school Early Decision."

"What does any of this have to do with Demonstrated Interest?" Michelle asked.

"Applying binding Early Decision is a great way to show interest in a college," Victoria said. "After all, if Jack applies Early Decision somewhere, he is committing to attend if he's accepted. It's hard to think of a stronger statement of interest in a school."

"What about the odds?" Michelle asked. "You said they're not always what they appear."

"You'll see a lot of statistics about Early Decision acceptance rates versus Regular Decision acceptance rates," Jon said. "For example, a school might have a 30 percent Early Decision acceptance rate and a 15 percent Regular Decision acceptance rate. That's why every year I have parents who tell me, 'We have to apply Early Decision to improve our chances.'"

"Isn't that the case?" Michelle asked.

"The acceptance rates by themselves don't give us enough information to draw that conclusion," Phil said. "The Early Decision applicant pool is often skewed to include a higher proportion of students with Hooks, like Legacy students or recruited athletes. What would be really useful to know is what the Early Decision acceptance rate is for students with Hooks versus students without Hooks, but colleges aren't forthcoming with that info."

"So Early Decision is a bad idea for Jack, then?" Michelle asked.

"Early Decision could be a good idea for Jack, but only under certain conditions," Victoria said. "First, the Early Decision school has to be his clear first choice. Second, he has to have visited the college, since there's no sense in committing to a school sight unseen. Third, he has to be comfortable never knowing what might have happened with his other applications, since he will have to withdraw all those other applications immediately if he is accepted Early Decision. If Jack meets all those conditions, then go for it!"

"The parents of one of my students were wrestling with this decision," Jon said. "The kid had strong numbers — 1500 on the SAT and a 4.9 weighted GPA — and solid extracurriculars — Key Club, soccer, and Boy Scouts — but no Hook. The parents told me after one of our sessions that they heard from a friend that Early Decision was necessary to improve their chances of getting into a 'good' school. They were thinking about Early Decision to Cornell. The only problem was that their son had never visited Cornell and wanted to stay in California. After some discussion and reflection, they scrapped the Early Decision plan and settled on applying to a few schools Early Action instead."

"Early Action?" Michelle asked. "What's that?"

"Early Action is similar to Early Decision," Victoria said. "It has the same early application deadline, usually around November 1st, and the same admission decision notification, usually around December 15th. But there are two important differences. First, unlike Early Decision, Early Action is non-binding. That means even if Jack applies Early Action to a school and gets accepted, he could always decide to go somewhere else.

Second, though Jack can only apply to one Early Decision school, he can apply to multiple Early Action schools. That means if he applies Early Action to five schools, he could have decisions for all five schools by mid-December. Not a bad way to start winter break!"

"Early Action sounds much better," Michelle said. "More flexibility. So why can't Jack just skip Early Decision and apply everywhere Early Action?"

"Not all schools offer Early Action," Phil said. "Many colleges, including many of the Top 25 Schools, only offer Early Decision. Some offer both Early Decision and Early Action. A few, including Harvard, Yale, Princeton, and Stanford, offer Single-Choice Early Action or Restrictive Early Action, which prevents the student from applying Early Action to other private universities. So Jack has to choose from whichever plans his colleges offer. It's not entirely up to him."

"Let's say a school on Jack's list offers Early Action," Michelle said. "Is there any reason *not* to apply Early Action?"

"Early Action schools won't see a student's first semester senior year grades," Jon said. "If the student has had a rough junior year, then those first semester senior year grades can boost his GPA and prove his grades are trending in the right direction. That's the main reason to skip Early Action and go for Regular Decision."

"That said, when my students already have solid junior year grades, I encourage them to apply to as many schools as possible Early Action," Victoria said. "Especially when the college in question is a Target School or a Safety School, it almost always makes sense to apply Early Action."

"I'll have to talk to Jack about Early Decision and Early Action," Michelle said.

"This was just practice, anyway," Phil said. "Here, take your poker chip back as a reminder." Phil picked the white and gold chip off the table and handed it to Michelle, who slipped it into her tote bag.

"There's also a practical reason for applying Early Action or Early Decision," Jon said. "Meeting a November 1st Early Action deadline or Early Decision deadline is the easiest way to accelerate the whole application timetable. The sooner Jack gets the first application in, the sooner he'll finish with all of them."

"It's only natural for you to review that first application two, three, four, five times," Phil said. "You'll want it to be perfect."

"Most families are nervous when they submit that first application, so sometimes they put it off," Victoria said. "But the sooner you submit the first application, the sooner everyone's nerves settle, and then you start to build up momentum, like 'We did the first one! Now let's do one more!'"

"Got it," Michelle said. "Jack will submit at least one application Early Decision or Early Action by November 1st."

As Michelle spoke the phrase, "Early Action," the violet door swung open, revealing a flight of bright violet steps.

"Almost there," Victoria said. "The violet steps are the last part of the Rainbow Road."

Interviewing

The group filed through the doorway and up onto the violet stairs. "So what's the last part of Demonstrated Interest?" Michelle asked.

"Hi there!" a voice called out from above. "Would you like to schedule an interview?"

"Barbie?" Victoria asked. "I thought you were down on the blue stairs leading tours with Ken. We didn't even see you pass us on the Stairway."

"I lost my access card to the doors on the Rainbow Road, so I had to hitch a ride up to the top on the Hyperloop and then run all the way back down. But I'm here now, so let's get started!"

"What's this interview you mentioned?" Michelle asked. "Is it required?"

"Well, for Heavenly U, an alumni interview will be optional but highly recommended," Barbie said.

"Interview policies vary widely from school to school," Victoria said. "Some are alumni interviews, some are interviews with a regional admissions rep when she visits your area, and some are on-campus interviews."

"The scheduling and timing of the interviews also vary," Phil said. "For some schools, the student has to request the interview, and for others, the school contacts the student. For some schools, every student gets an interview, and for others, space is limited. For some schools, interviews are in the fall, and for others it's early winter. For some schools, the interview is informative, and for others it's evaluative. You have to check the college's websites for details."

"At least for Heavenly U, the interviews are optional," Michelle said.

"But highly recommended," Barbie said.

"I tell my students that optional means optional only if they don't want to get in," Victoria said. "But if you don't want to get in, then why are you applying?"

"The main exception to our 'optional-doesn't-mean-optional' rule is if the student won't come across well in an interview," Jon said. "Some students are socially awkward. Maybe they can't maintain eye contact, or maybe they only give one-sentence answers. For students who take a little longer to warm up to, the risk of a bad interview could outweigh the risk of no interview. So use your judgment."

"How big of a factor is the interview?" Michelle asked.

"Usually it's a minor factor," Victoria said. "Alumni might meet with applicants and write up a brief summary of the interview, including some comments on the applicant's academic ability, extracurricular activities, and personal appeal. The summary goes into the applicant's admissions file, which alumni don't usually see. A bad interview might cause a college to scrutinize a promising applicant more carefully, but a good interview won't make up for terrible grades."

"Remember, though, if you're not sure how much the interview matters, you can always check Section C7 of the Common Data Set, that survey we mentioned that most of the colleges fill out," Phil said.

"There's a lot you can do to help Jack prep for his interview," Jon said. "When I was an alumni interviewer for Harvard, I saw some baffling, avoidable mistakes, like arriving late. I always remind my students to arrive early, make eye contact, give a firm handshake, and introduce themselves with a smile."

"Isn't that obvious?" Michelle asked.

"To us, yes, and to many students, yes," Jon said. "But for some students, this is the first time they've gone through a formal interview process. It never hurts to cover stuff that seems obvious."

"What about the actual interview questions, though?" Michelle asked.

"Honestly, if Jack has done a good job including anecdotes in his application essays, reviewing those essays should prepare him to answer almost any question that comes his way," Victoria said.

"He should be able to talk about his favorite classes, the ways he spends his time in activities or helping at home, any meaningful experiences or challenges he has faced, and any books he has read recently," Phil said.

"When I prep my students for interviews, I just ask them these questions and let them ramble," Jon said. "Then when they finally finish, I ask what their main point is and what they want their interviewer to know about them. Then I ask them to answer the question again — and again —

until they can give a concise answer while staying relaxed. It often takes five or more times before they find their groove."

"Right," Victoria said. "The problem is that most students want to stop after practicing a question once. They feel self-conscious once they realize how often they say, 'um,' or 'like,' or once they realize their response doesn't sound natural or that they haven't even answered the question."

"I tell my students that prepping for interviews is like practicing for a big game or a big recital," Phil said. "You want the preparation to be more grueling than the actual event. But like Victoria said, it's uncomfortable, so it takes some prodding. If the student wants to practice on his own, he can always video himself answering questions, or he can answer questions in front of a mirror."

"Though practice is important, you can't let Jack lose sight of the real goal of the interview," Jon said.

"Which is what?" Michelle asked.

"To establish a rapport so that the interviewer likes him," Jon said. "The faster the interviewer moves from rigid question-and-answer to free-flowing conversation, the better. And Jack should come prepared with some questions of his own for the interviewer."

"If he has time, he can even google the interviewer's name to get some background info and find possible shared interests," Phil said. "LinkedIn is a good source of information, too."

"The questions Jack asks the interviewer don't have to be super-complicated," Jon said. "He can always ask, 'What do you know now about the school that you wished you knew before you started?' or 'What surprised you about the school?' or 'What advice would you give me as I start college and try to figure out my career?' Anything to make the interview more conversational works."

"Right," Victoria said. "Most people want to help out, so when you ask someone for advice, you tap into that person's natural desire to be helpful. Then the person being asked for advice thinks, 'What a smart person, asking me for advice. I like this person!' Students can easily use this idea in their college interviews."

"If the interview happens early enough in the calendar year, Jack can think about working what he learns about the school from the interview into his essay," Phil said. "Especially if he won't get the chance to visit the school in person."

"Most of all, Jack should relax, impossible though as that might sound," Jon said. "The interviewers love their schools, and they want others to love them, too, so they're not out to make students miserable. Especially the alumni interviewers who are volunteering their time."

"Well," Barbie said, "that's a lot to consider, but if you can coach Jack through these points, he'll be more than ready for his interview." Just then, Barbie's phone buzzed. "Oops, that's Ken. Three screaming-in-fear emoji. That's how he lets me know something's wrong. Probably called some VIP 'dude' again. I'd better check on him. See you all later!" Barbie sprinted down the stairs in search of her wayward colleague.

"Bye!" Victoria called after Barbie as she turned to Michelle and the group continued up the violet steps. "Many schools' applications ask students to list all forms of contact they have had with the school. That will be Jack's chance to show the school how deep his interest is, so make sure he is as detailed as possible about how he has connected with the school."

"Sometimes, Demonstrated Interest continues even after the application is submitted," Jon said. "If Jack is deferred or waitlisted, he can demonstrate interest by sending update letters on recent academic and extracurricular accomplishments or by obtaining additional Letters of Rec. Even a counselor's Letter of Recommendation confirming that the school is the student's first choice can demonstrate interest."

"There are lots of ways to demonstrate interest in a school," Victoria said as the group continued climbing the stairs. "Responding to marketing material, signing up for the school's email list, following the school on social media, getting to know the admissions rep, visiting campus, applying early, and interviewing are all good possibilities."

"Even for the schools that don't count Demonstrated Interest as an admissions factor, it still makes sense to get to know the school better, like by signing up for the email list," Phil said. "At worst, that will help Jack write a better Why This College Essay. At best, it will confirm for him that this school really is a good fit for him."

"For schools that do consider Demonstrated Interest, don't get trapped in the mindset that you have to show interest in every way possible or else it's not worth doing at all," Jon said. "It's not all or nothing."

"You could say that about the whole college application process," Phil said. "Sure, there will always be some other parent or student out there doing more. But your goal is to keep Jack's focus on what he can do, not on what everyone else is doing."

Michelle and the three College Fates reached the final violet step and climbed up onto a landing with white marble floors. "That's it for the Rainbow Road and Demonstrated Interest," Jon said.

Victoria pointed to a sign attached to the railing on the landing which read, "College Heaven: 4,422 Steps."

"More than halfway there!" Victoria said.

Words of Wisdom from the Boss

"Demonstrating interest in a college includes responding to marketing materials, signing up for the email list, following the school on social media, cultivating relationships with admissions reps, visiting campus, applying Early Action or Early Decision, and interviewing. Though not every school tracks Demonstrated Interest, it is always a good idea for your child to get to know the schools on his list as well as possible. The more your child demonstrates interest in various schools, the more confident he will be in his assessment of which schools are good fits for him."

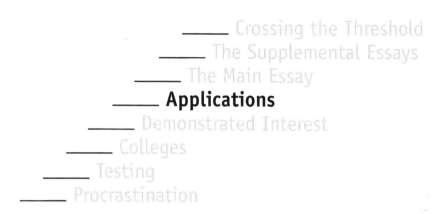

"What's that sound?" Michelle asked, looking around the landing.

In the middle of the landing stood an eight-foot-high grandfather clock finished in oak with an arched pediment. The circular clockface was of a golden tone, with Roman numerals near the outer edge to mark the hours. In the middle of the clockface was an etching of a fire-breathing dragon chasing a small figure up a stairway. The glass door at the bottom of the grandfather clock housed brass chimes and a brass pendulum. As Michelle and the three College Fates stopped to catch their breath, they could hear the tick tock as the pendulum swung back and forth, back and forth, ticking away the seconds.

"I've never seen a grandfather clock with a dragon before," Michelle said.

"You already know about Draggin and procrastination," Jon said.

"There's nothing like an actual ticking clock to create a sense of urgency," Phil said. "Real application deadlines are the fastest way to get students moving."

"That's why we're big on having our students apply Early Action or Early Decision to at least one school," Victoria said. "That November 1st early deadline has magical anti-procrastination powers."

The group fell silent again, listening to the ticktock.

"Before we head out from here, I'd like you to have this," Victoria said. Victoria pulled from her robes a red analog alarm clock with twin bells and a strong tick-tick pulse and handed it to Michelle. Michelle's hands dropped a couple inches as she received it.

"This thing is heavy!" Michelle said.

"Just a friendly reminder to mind the time," Jon said. "So are you ready?"

"For what?" Michelle asked.

"This next stretch is what we call the 'Deadline Dash,'" Phil said, leading the group behind the grandfather clock to the next section of the Stairway.

Application Deadlines

"You have 184 seconds to make it to the next landing," Victoria said.

"Is this really necessary?" Michelle asked. "I get it, don't procrastinate, start early. And why 184 seconds?"

"That's the number of days in college application season, from July 1st to January 1st," Victoria said.

"What if I don't make it in time?" Michelle asked.

"I think you know the answer," Jon said.

"Draggin?" Michelle asked.

"The last few parents on the Stairway have finished the Deadline Dash without any trouble," Phil said. "Which is great for them, but..."

"Let's just say their success has left Draggin a bit hungry," Victoria said. "She can't wait to pick off the next straggler."

Michelle's eyes widened. She glanced from Victoria to Jon to Phil and then back to Victoria. The three College Fates remained silent, their faces frozen in serious expressions.

Then Jon smiled. "Oh all right, we're just messing with you. We haven't actually lost anyone to Draggin on the Deadline Dash," he said. "But some parents have definitely had their clothes singed."

Michelle inhaled and exhaled slowly. "OK, I'm ready," she said.

"When the grandfather clock chimes, you start running," Victoria said. "We'll be right behind you." No sooner had Victoria finished speaking than the clock began to chime.

"Run!" the three College Fates yelled at Michelle. And run she did.

The Stairway's handrails were covered with hanging clocks ticking and clanging in unknowable rhythms and syncopations. "There's the first checkpoint, July 4th," Jon called out as Michelle passed a clock with the Declaration of Independence painted on its face.

"That's the latest Jack needs to start working on his application essays!" Phil said. "First step to freedom."

"Application essays?" Michelle asked over her shoulder. "I thought there was only one!"

"We'll get into that later, keep running!" Jon said as the group kept moving through the gantlet of timekeeping devices.

Michelle ran past a clock with an intricate painting of a red schoolhouse on its face. "Second checkpoint, Labor Day!" Victoria shouted.

"Ask teachers and counselors for Letters of Recommendation," Phil said.

"Jack will barely be back in school by Labor Day. That soon?"

"Teachers and counselors often have their own student questionnaires," Jon said.

"Sometimes they ask for essays," Victoria said. "It can be like filling out a whole other college application."

"Jack has to figure out those Letters of Rec as soon as possible, but definitely by Labor Day," Phil said.

"I need to rest for a few seconds," Michelle said, leaning over and putting her hands on her knees. The Stairway shuddered, and a double fireball passed over the group from below. The group looked back to see Draggin amble across the landing below and knock over the grandfather clock. Then, with a single breath of flames, Draggin set the clock on fire before looking up at Michelle and roaring. "Done resting!" Michelle said, sprinting up the Stairway. "Where's the next checkpoint?"

"There!" Jon said, pointing to a clock with an orange jack-o-lantern clockface.

"Third checkpoint, Halloween!" Victoria said.

"Most Early Decision and Early Action deadlines are November 1st. Early applications should all be submitted by Halloween," Phil said.

"At the latest!" Jon said. "One more to go!"

"There," Phil said as the group ran past a clock the face of which was decorated with a silhouette of two people kissing. The clock's chimes played "Auld Lang Syne" amid the din of the ticking and clanging.

"New Year's Eve?" Michelle asked.

"January 1st is the Regular Decision deadline for most colleges, so yes, all the rest of Jack's applications should be in by December 31st," Victoria said.

"Time?" Jon asked.

"20 seconds left," Phil said. "19, 18…"

At the next landing, just a few steps above, a blue finish line tape stretched across the Stairway. Michelle ran through it, and the ticking and clanging from all the clocks on the Deadline Dash stopped. The only sound was a snort from Draggin, who had paused on the Stairway below and was now eyeing the climbers. Two tendrils of smoke rose from her nostrils. She hung her head, turned around, and thudded back down the Stairway.

Michelle placed both hands on top of her head, breathing quickly and deeply as she paced around the landing. At the far side stood a hedge that rose at least 20 feet above the landing, blocking the view of the next section of the Stairway.

"So what do you remember about the deadlines?" Victoria asked.

"I have to catch my breath," Michelle said.

"Essays?" Jon asked.

"July 4th," Michelle said.

"Asking about Letters of Rec?" Jon asked.

"Labor Day," Michelle said.

"Early applications?" Jon asked.

"By Halloween," Michelle said.

"Regular Decision apps?" Jon asked.

"New Year's Eve," Michelle said.

"Perfect!" Victoria said.

"That's fine for the deadlines, but what about filling out the application?" Michelle said. "I don't even know which forms to look at."

"You read our minds," Jon said. "Let's head over to the hedge. There's something we want you to see."

Application Forms

Jon walked over toward the hedge on the other side of the landing, and the others followed. "I know there's an entrance in here somewhere." Jon thrust his arms into the hedge and shook the branches. "No, hmm… Maybe over here." Jon moved to the left and tried again. "Aha, yes, here it is." Jon pushed the branches apart just enough for the others to squeeze through. "In we go."

On the other side of the hedge, the group found itself in a small, square clearing surrounded by more hedges. Each hedge had an opening leading down another path. "What happened to the Stairway?" Michelle asked.

"The Boss, well, as much as she likes the nice hardscape of the Stairway, she also enjoys some greenery," Victoria said. "There's a special place in her heart for gardens, I guess. Some local high school students were trying to figure out their Eagle Scout project, so she agreed to let them do a Stairway beautification project. Thought it would calm the parents on the Stairway. There's nothing like a little nature for relaxation."

"So we just wander around?" Michelle asked.

"Well, technically, you wander around," Phil said. "We've been here hundreds of times, so it only takes us a couple minutes."

"You're leaving me?" Michelle asked.

"If there's a bustle in your hedgerow, don't be alarmed now," Jon said. Then the three College Fates rushed through the opening to the right and disappeared around the corner.

"Hey, wait!" Michelle yelled. But they were gone. "Seriously?" she muttered to herself.

The three College Fates exited the maze within two minutes, as expected, and found some outdoor seating at Heavenly Grounds, the café conveniently located at the end of the maze. The only restaurant on the Stairway, it was known for its freshly roasted artisanal fair trade coffee and tasty organic desserts. Jon ordered his coffee black, Victoria went for an Americano, and Phil decided on a pumpkin latte. The three College Fates found a table outside on the patio and sat down to wait for Michelle. An hour later, she emerged from the maze holding a sheaf of papers and stalked over to the three College Fates.

"You made it!" Victoria said.

"No thanks to all of you!" Michelle said. She thrust the papers down on the table, removed a small twig from her hair, and brushed her bangs out of her eyes.

"Something to drink?" Phil asked.

"That's the least you can do," Michelle said, pulling out a chair and taking a seat at the table between Jon and Victoria. "Just a cup of iced coffee would be fine, thank you."

"What did you find?" Victoria asked.

"Do you know how confusing all this is?" Michelle asked. "Here's the Common Application." Michelle set a few pages down in one stack on the table. "Here's the Coalition Application." Michelle set down another few pages on the table. "Here's the University of California application." Michelle made another stack on the table. "And these," she said, waving another bundle of papers in the air, "are all the Common Application supplements and the individual school-based applications. This is absurd!"

"Aren't you glad you figured that out now instead of later?" Jon said.

"It is a bit much," Victoria said. "The Common App helps reduce the workload, but since most Common App schools have their own Supplemental Essays, most families are surprised to find how much there is left to do."

"Public school applications get complicated, too," Jon said. "Many public schools have their own system-wide application forms. Some are on the Common App. More and more are gravitating toward the Coalition App. And many others are on multiple application platforms."

"Once you have Jack's College List, you'll definitely want to go to each college's website to see which application forms it accepts," Victoria said.

"Forms, plural?" Michelle asked.

"Some colleges accept more than one form," Jon said. "Jack should only submit one, though."

"If Jack has the choice between using a school-specific application and a more general application such as the Common App, he should use the school-specific application," Victoria said. "A college has its own application form for a reason — that's often the form it prefers."

Phil returned to the table. "Here you go," Phil said, setting the iced coffee down on the table in front of Michelle between all the stacks of paper. "And here's dessert for us to share." Phil placed a plate with a big slice of pie à la mode at the middle of the table, passed out forks, and sat down at the table across from Michelle.

"Ooh, what's this?" Michelle asked.

"Apple-cation pie," Phil said.

"Seriously?" Michelle asked, raising her eyebrows. "Apple-cation pie?"

"After the maze was done, another Eagle Scout came through and proposed planting an apple orchard. At first, the Boss was reluctant. Bad memories of fruit, she said. But that Eagle Scout was so persistent that eventually she gave in, and we're glad she did. Now every fall, Heavenly Grounds uses apples from that orchard to make pie," Victoria said. "Baked fresh daily. We told her apple-cation pie was such a dad joke, and she just said, 'It's the 21st century. A woman can tell a dad joke if she wants.' We weren't about to argue. Her point is that the Stairway to College Heaven isn't all drudgery and dragons. There are some sweet moments, too."

"Dig in, before the ice cream melts," Jon said. Michelle and the three College Fates each took a bite of the apple-cation pie.

"Delicious!" Michelle said. "There's nothing like warm apple pie."

"With vanilla ice cream," Jon said. "Apple-cation pie is fine by itself, but the ice cream puts it over the top."

"That's true of college applications, too," Phil said, lowering his fork and looking toward Michelle.

"Vanilla ice cream?" Michelle asked.

"I mean the extras," Phil said, picking up the papers and gathering them into a single pile. "These applications are important, but you can't skip the extras."

"What extras?" Michelle asked.

Application Requirements

"The Application Requirements beyond the application itself," Phil said.

"You have to check each college's website to confirm its Application Requirements," Victoria said. "But a few common ones come to mind."

"Sending ACT, SAT, and SAT Subject Test scores is one," Phil said. "For any scores that Jack chooses to report or that the college requires him to report, he'll have to send score reports through the College Board or ACT website."

"Sending transcripts is another one," Jon said. "If a college asks for transcripts, Jack has to send the transcript for any school where he has taken a high school or college course for credit.

"Even if he just took a single course there, like for summer school," Phil added.

"Jack may self-report his GPA on the application, but most schools will require an official transcript," Victoria said. "Once senior year starts, you'll want to remind him to drop by his counselor's office to see what the procedure is. Most schools will require a mid-year report with first semester senior year grades, too."

"Letters of Recommendation we mentioned, too, during the Deadline Dash," Phil said. "Yes, asking by Labor Day is good, but these take some time to follow up on."

"Not to mention some time to prepare," Victoria said. "Jack's a junior, so now is the perfect time for him to cultivate those relationships with teachers."

"This early?" Michelle asked.

"Jack's probably going to need two teacher Letters of Recommendation," Jon said. "These should be from teachers of core academic subjects, meaning English, history, math, science, or a language other than English. Ideally, these will be honors or AP teachers."

"Colleges look to teacher Letters of Rec because teachers are best positioned to describe what kind of student Jack is," Phil said. "That's why Jack should strive to connect with his teachers."

"Getting good grades is a start, and participating in class helps, too," Victoria said. "It can be as simple as asking an intelligent question or taking a risk and being the first to answer a question."

"Jack can go beyond class time, too," Jon said. "If the class is something Jack is genuinely interested in, he can do some extra reading at home and talk to the teacher about it outside of class. One of my students read an excerpt of Walt Whitman's book *Leaves of Grass* in English class on Monday. He liked it so much that he bought it on Amazon that night, and when it arrived on Tuesday, he stayed up all night reading it. Then on Wednesday, he went and talked to his teacher about it at lunch. Do I think that helped the teacher write a better Letter of Rec? Absolutely!"

"Just like with the interview, the goal is a rapport," Phil said. "Teachers end up sacrificing personal time to write these letters, and no one can force them to write them a certain way. So it's crucial for Jack to have built up lots of good will with whichever teachers he intends to ask."

"This all sounds pretty calculated," Michelle said.

"There is some strategy, yes," Jon said, "but it really only works when the student has genuine affection for the subject matter and genuine respect for the teacher. Jack could fake it, but that's not what we're advocating. We're saying, 'Hey, find an academic subject that really interests you, and go get to know your teacher who is interested in that same subject!'"

"Another approach is for Jack to get involved with a school club one of his teachers sponsors," Victoria said. "That way, the teacher really gets to know Jack and has a wider range of experiences to write about. For example, if the teacher advisor for Model United Nations also teaches AP US History, that's the perfect teacher for a future political science student to get to know better."

"Don't get me wrong, it's awkward for most students to ask for Letters of Rec," Jon said. "But it's way less awkward if the student already has a warm relationship with the teacher."

"This is so much work!" Michelle said. "It's not just the application process you're talking about. It's the whole high school experience." Michelle sighed.

"All the investment is worth it," Phil said. "When a kid is applying to selective schools, the GPA and SAT and ACT scores look pretty similar from one student to the next, so the Letters of Recommendation — especially the teacher Letters of Rec — take on a bigger role in helping students stand out."

"You want to make it as easy as possible for the people writing his Letters of Rec to do a great job," Jon said. "When teachers or counselors send out a questionnaire or brag packet asking for Jack's accomplishments, interests, and values, make sure Jack doesn't just write two-sentence responses. He should take the time to write out anecdotes, including specific moments from class or activities that he found meaningful, and why."

"The more great material Jack gives his teachers and counselor, the easier it is for them to write great letters," Phil said.

"Writing detailed responses to questionnaires is tough, but so is following up with teachers and counselors," Victoria said. "It will be October, and Jack will be looking at his November 1st deadlines, and his teachers won't necessarily have submitted all their Letters of Rec — they're busy with class and a million other things, too — and you and Jack will be stressed that the letters aren't in yet. But all you can do is have Jack follow up in person or by email. I always like to say, 'Be politely persistent.'"

"When my students aren't sure what to say, I tell them to ask their teachers, 'Is there anything else you need from me to finish my Letter of Recommendation?'" Jon said. "That's more tactful than asking, 'Did you finish yet?' Not that Jack would ever say it that way."

"No matter how awkward it is, Jack shouldn't be shy about following up," Phil said. "The last thing you want is to realize on Halloween that the letter he needs for his November 1st early application isn't done."

"Teachers and counselors have a huge workload already, and getting Letters of Rec done is madness," Jon said. "So remind Jack to thank them. Not just by email. But in person, too. There's nothing wrong with a thank-you gift or a thank-you card."

"So beyond the application, I need to make sure that SAT, ACT, and SAT Subject Test reports, transcripts, and Letters of Rec all get submitted," Michelle said. "Any other requirements that should be on my radar?"

"Visual or performing arts students, engineering students, or even business students might be required to submit samples of their work through SlideRoom," Jon said.

"SlideRoom?" Michelle asked.

"Application forms such as the Common App aren't really set up to handle student Portfolios," Phil said. "SlideRoom is a website customized to handle samples of student work, so many colleges use it in conjunction with their application form."

"Some schools do accept Portfolios even if the Portfolio isn't related to the student's intended major," Jon said. "For example, a school might allow a biology major to submit a photography Portfolio. Taking advantage of this option can boost an application by showing another dimension of the student's interests."

"At some schools, the deadline for Portfolio submissions is even earlier than the Early Action or Early Decision deadline," Victoria said. "You might see a November 1st deadline for Early Action, but an October 15th deadline for Portfolios. Or the Regular Decision deadline might be January 1st, but the Portfolio deadline could be December 1st. It really varies, so you have to check each school's website."

"Remember those interviews we told you about on the Rainbow Road when we were discussing Demonstrated Interest?" Phil asked. "Those are optional for some schools but mandatory for others, and deadlines vary from school to school."

"Never make assumptions about a college's Application Requirements," Victoria said. "Always check the school's website directly. If something isn't clear, don't shrug it off. Ask Jack to email or call the admissions office for clarification."

Michelle chewed on a bite of apple-cation pie with ice cream. "Here, take the last bite," Phil said, sliding the plate toward Michelle.

"Thanks," Michelle said. "I thought there would be an easier way. Checking each college's website sounds annoying."

"It's the only way to have peace of mind," Victoria said. "One of the best ways parents can help their kids is by creating a spreadsheet or checklist with all the Application Requirements. Then you won't wake up the morning after the deadline wondering if you missed something."

"Pay extra attention to Application Requirements that Jack needs others' help to complete, like Letters of Recommendation," Jon said. "Jack should start coordinating those items as early as possible so he doesn't have to rush around at the deadline."

"If you set up a spreadsheet and make sure Jack gets an early start on items that require outside help, he'll have it under control," Phil said.

"Should we get going?" Victoria asked. "This was a great snack, but we're going to be hungry again soon, and there's no more food until we get to College Heaven."

"Victoria's right," Jon said. "We should keep moving."

"Do I need to keep all these?" Michelle asked, picking up the application pages scattered across the table.

"No, just recycle them over there," Victoria said, pointing to the green recycling bin behind Michelle. "All the applications are online, anyway." Michelle and the three College Fates rose from the patio table. Michelle recycled the applications she had acquired in the maze while Jon cleared the table and threw away all the trash.

The group headed out of the patio area over to the next section of the Stairway. Along the railing was a sign: "College Heaven: 2,827 Steps."

Words of Wisdom from the Boss

"The most important point about college applications is that each college has its own deadlines, forms, and requirements. The best way to figure out what a college needs is to check that college's website. If something is unclear, ask your child to email or call the college's admissions office. One of the most useful things you can do to help your child stay organized is to create a spreadsheet to keep track of Application Requirements. Once you have all the information in one place, you will know you have not overlooked anything, and you will be able to relax a little."

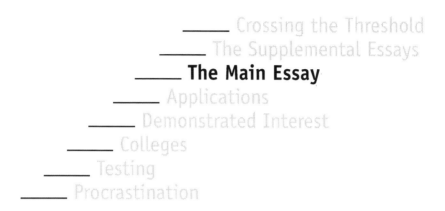

"What's left?" Michelle asked as the group resumed its climb up the Stairway.

"The application essays," Jon said. Michelle stopped short and then inhaled slowly. "We'll start with what we call the Main Essay."

"People call it lots of different names," Victoria said. "The 'personal statement,' the 'Common App essay,' or just the 'application essay.' This is the essay where Jack takes 500 to 650 words to say something important about himself."

"The wording of the essay prompts for the Main Essay varies depending on whether we're looking at the Common App, the Coalition App, or some other application," Phil said, "but the student's goal is still the same: show colleges what a great kid he is."

"He is a great kid," Michelle said, pausing and turning to Jon. "Just not a great writer."

"That's what most parents tell us," Victoria said. "Fortunately, you don't have to be a great writer to write a great essay."

"That doesn't make any sense," Michelle said.

"Have you seen ads for those companies that deliver boxes with ingredients and recipes, and all you have to do is follow the instructions to make a gourmet dinner?" Phil asked.

"Sure," Michelle said. "Last week I got one of those and made barbecue chicken turnovers with cone cabbage and apple slaw. It was delicious. No leftovers."

"And you're not a master chef?" Phil asked.

"I know my way around the kitchen, and I have my go-to list of family favorites," Michelle said, "but it's not like I have any professional training."

"It's the same with writing," Victoria said. "Jack doesn't have to be a master writer to create something memorable."

"Ready?" Phil asked, pointing up at the next section of the Stairway, where the wrought-iron railing gave way to ten-foot-high cinder block walls and the Stairway narrowed to allow only one person to pass at a time.

"I don't know about this," Michelle said as they neared the start of the walled section of the Stairway. The walls cast a shadow over the group, and a cold wind whistled down the Stairway. "This feels like a prison."

"That's exactly what the Boss was going for here!" Victoria said. "She wanted to prepare parents for how uncomfortable writing can be."

"Isn't there another way?" Michelle asked, turning around and craning her neck down toward the sunnier stretches of the Stairway below.

Draggin roared and sent three fiery rings up the Stairway and over the prison walls. Michelle glanced at Jon, eyebrows raised. "Sometimes Draggin gets bored with fireballs. Fire rings seem to be this month's project," Jon said as he shrugged his shoulders.

"The sooner you get started on the Main Essay, the sooner you'll be done with it," Victoria said.

"I suppose," Michelle said. "But one of you has to go first."

"It's bad, but not as bad as you think," Phil said as he led the group into the narrow passageway. "The first step is to understand the problem."

Understanding the Problem

"Take a look at the walls," Jon said. The cinder block walls were covered with posters.

"What are these?" Michelle asked. "I can make out eyes, noses, and mouths, but they're all pixelated."

"These are student portraits," Victoria said.

"They all look the same!" Michelle said. "I can't tell them apart."

"What about this one?" Jon asked, pointing to a picture on the left-hand wall.

"What about it?" Michelle asked.

"That's Jack!" Victoria said.

"No way!" Michelle said. "That can't be my Jack. He looks like all the others!"

"That's the first thing you have to understand about the Main Essay," Jon said. "Most Main Essays are so low-resolution that the portrait of one student looks the same as the next."

"This will never work," Michelle said. "I want colleges to remember Jack. His Main Essay has to be a high-resolution portrait. I want that thing looking like it was shot on a full-frame DSLR, not an iPhone 4."

"Exactly right," Victoria said. "Come on, we'll show you how to make that happen." Victoria beckoned Michelle to continue up the Stairway.

Brainstorming with Adjectives

A few steps above, the walls changed from gray cinder block to black granite that was polished to a perfect smoothness broken only by words carved into its surface.

Michelle raised both her hands above her shoulders, one to each side, as she ran her fingertips over the inscriptions. "There must be thousands of words here," she said.

"These are the Walls of Adjectives," Phil said. "This is where we ask all parents and students to start their essay brainstorming."

"Shouldn't we be starting with the essay prompt instead of adjectives?" Michelle asked. "I don't want Jack to waste time writing something off-topic."

"When we're talking about the Main Essay, the prompts are so broad that nearly any topic will work," Jon said. "We start with the student, not the prompt."

"Even the Common App often has a 'topic of your choice' prompt," Phil said. "We begin by asking parents, 'Which three adjectives best describe your child?'"

"That's easy," Michelle said. "Jack is curious, caring, and stubborn."

"Good," Phil said. "Let's keep going."

As the group left the Walls of Adjectives behind, the black granite gave way to white stucco. Affixed to each wall, from the very bottom to the very top, was a grid of square, white cubbies, each one 12 inches by 12 inches, like something out of an IKEA catalog. Inside of each, there was an object.

Moving from Adjectives to Memories

"This is the Passage of Memories," Jon said. "Adjectives are good starting points for brainstorming, but they can't carry the Main Essay on their own. They have to be linked to memories."

"Any adjective you can use to describe Jack has been sharpened and shaped through experience," Victoria said. "Once you have some adjectives in mind, it's time to take a few minutes to remember which experiences developed those qualities."

"What are all these cubbies for, then?" Michelle asked.

"The Boss filled them with objects that might help you remember moments from Jack's life," Phil said. "She thought a tactile approach would be easier than trying to write a list from scratch."

"Many of these cubbies hold objects related to Jack's life at home," Jon said as he pointed up at them. "You'll find some family photographs, too, including some with your parents." Michelle retrieved a photo from one of the cubbies.

"Oh, this one's from our trip to Mount Rushmore when he was ten," Michelle said. "It's the last family vacation we did with my dad. Jack spent the whole car ride reading us trivia about the US presidents. The kid was obsessed. Even now, I see that same focus whenever Jack finds something new that grabs his attention."

"That memory does a great job proving Jack's curiosity," Victoria said. "For the Main Essay, you'll want more recent examples, probably from high school, but that's the right idea."

Michelle placed the photo back in its cubby, and the group kept walking, with Michelle pausing occasionally to remove, inspect, and replace various objects that caught her eye.

"I didn't expect to find this here," Michelle said, holding up a hospital bracelet for the three College Fates to see. "This is from his sophomore year when I was discharged from the hospital. I was on the way to pick up Jack's little sister, Hannah, from school when another car ran a red light and smashed into us. I broke my leg in three places, and for the next couple months, Jack had to help with everything from getting Hannah ready for school to helping me make dinner to driving me to and from doctor appointments. It was tough, especially when my husband was out of town for work, but Jack never complained. He always wanted to make sure Hannah and I were taken care of."

"That's a perfect memory to show his compassionate side," Jon said. "I would encourage him to write about that experience."

"Some of these cubbies hold objects that relate to Jack's extracurricular activities and life outside the home, too," Phil said as the group continued walking.

"Here's a gavel," Michelle said. "That must be for Mock Trial. Jack was paired with another kid who put in zero time and effort into researching and practicing. Jack's team got destroyed in competitions. I was so mad. I kept telling Jack to talk to the club advisor and ask for a new partner. But Jack being Jack, he refused. He thought he should just deal with it, and nothing I said would convince him otherwise. He can be so stubborn sometimes."

"Whichever adjectives you and Jack decide to explore, you're bound to find some memories that show Jack putting that quality into action, like the one you just mentioned," Victoria said.

"The range of memories you can use for the Main Essay is nearly boundless," Phil said. "They could relate to Jack's leadership, creativity, greatest talent, educational opportunities, educational barriers, significant challenges, favorite subject, community, or anything else that makes him special. Keep an open mind!"

"Even personal family circumstances are fine to write about to illustrate the adjectives you choose," Jon said. "We've had students write about divorce, illness, anorexia, sexual assault, depression, and more. We're not saying Jack has to write about something like that if he doesn't want to, but he should consider the possibility."

"Being honest about meaningful experiences — even very personal ones — provides context that helps colleges appreciate a student's achievements," Victoria said.

"Do you mind if I take a few minutes to wander by myself?" Michelle asked.

"Not at all," Jon said. "Explore your memories of Jack, and you can catch up with us at the next landing." The three College Fates strode up the Stairway, leaving Michelle to ponder in the Passage of Memories.

Avoiding Fall Hell

A few minutes later, Michelle caught up to the three College Fates on a small landing about the size of an elevator and enclosed by silver, metallic walls. "Find anything interesting?" Victoria asked.

"More than I expected," Michelle said as the group left the landing and continued its ascent past the metallic walls. "I think there's plenty for him to write about, but…" Her voice trailed off.

"But what?" Phil asked.

"I'm really not looking forward to this conversation with Jack about all these adjectives and memories," Michelle said. "He's not the most talkative guy, especially with me lately. It's not like when he was little. Can I just let him figure this out on his own? I mean, the 12th grade English teachers at Jack's school all have their students write drafts over the summer, and then the teacher and other students give feedback in the fall."

Draggin roared from below, and the group quickened its pace ever so slightly.

"If you let Jack wait until fall to start the Main Essay, you'll end up in Fall Hell," Jon said.

"Fall Hell?" Michelle asked.

"You can't see it from up here on the Stairway, but Fall Hell is just over the horizon," Phil said. "If you think the Stairway is bad, let's hope you never find yourself trying to escape Fall Hell. It's a giant pit, very hot because of the lava bubbling up at the bottom. Parent and child are shackled together, and the only way out is up the Eliminator, a 66.6-mile treadmill ramp at a 20 percent incline."

"Sometimes, on a quiet fall night up here on the Stairway, when the breeze dies down, you can hear the wails of anguish from the legions of parents and students stuck on the Eliminator who wish they had finished the Main Essay the summer before senior year," Jon said. "But that's what happens when you procrastinate. Students always underestimate their fall workload. It's not easy to balance AP courses and college applications."

Michelle frowned. "That sounds awful!" she said. "I want Jack to start early, but I know how this will play out. I'll tell Jack to start writing. He'll give it a try. Then he'll tell me, 'I don't know what else to write,' and we'll be stuck. What do I say then?"

"Tell him confusion about what to write is normal," Jon said. "Many kids, especially the good students, expect to compose an essay that is insightful, personal, and organized within a day or two. When that doesn't happen, they start to panic. They wonder what's wrong with them."

"What's wrong with them is that their expectations of how good writing happens are completely unrealistic," Phil said. "Having some adjectives and memories in mind is just 10 percent of it. The other 90 percent is typing out anything that's remotely related."

"Confusion is good," Victoria said. "When a student already knows exactly what he wants to say, he usually ends up with the obvious and clichéd essay that's a variation of 'I did this' or 'I learned this,' and his essay sounds like thousands of others. That's how kids end up with the low-resolution, pixelated portraits like those posters you saw earlier."

"Remind Jack that no one gets the Main Essay right on the first try," Jon said. "Trial and error are always part of the process. It's like the Boss and this Stairway. Wise as she is, she once had us build a tunnel full of vampire bats, which turned out… Well, let's just say the vampire bats are gone now. Mistakes are unavoidable. Tell Jack there will be moments when he feels like he has nothing to write, or like nothing he has written is any good. Make sure he knows that doubt and uncertainty are part of writing. Otherwise, he might get discouraged."

"At the beginning of the writing process, the only measure of success is the number of words Jack writes," Victoria said. "It's all about quantity."

"We're almost to the Monkey Gate!" Phil said. "That should help you see what it takes to get started."

Writing Fast, Writing Lots

"The Monkey Gate?" Michelle asked. "You mean that monstrosity?" Michelle pointed up ahead, where a metal gate with no visible handles blocked the Stairway. Atop the gate two mechanical monkeys sat facing each other across a table, with a typewriter in front of each monkey. To the left of the gate was a shallow alcove with a table, a typewriter, and a small electronic scoreboard that displayed a red numeral *0*.

"You call it a monstrosity," Jon said, "but the Boss calls it art."

"We used to cover the importance of writing as much as possible as fast as possible in a PowerPoint presentation with 82 slides, perfectly formatted," Victoria said.

"When the Boss learned that our presentation was inducing spontaneous narcolepsy at a rate of 44 percent, she couldn't take it anymore," Phil said.

"She told us to create some kinetic sculptures to keep the parents engaged," Jon said. "One of my students had made two robots for an engineering competition, so we commissioned her to make a couple robot monkeys for the Stairway, and then we installed them on top of this gate.

"The one on the right in the green jacket and green fez is Speedy," Jon said. As Michelle listened, Speedy's mechanical paws were clacking out words on the typewriter at the maniacal pace of 231 words per minute.

"And that one over there in the red jacket and red fez is Slowpoke," Phil said, "but we call him Poky." Poky's paws meandered over the keyboard at a leisurely pace of nine words per minute.

Just then, Speedy grabbed a completed page from the typewriter, crumpled it up, and threw it off the gate. It came to rest at Michelle's feet. She knelt down, picked it up, smoothed it out, and started to read. "This stuff barely makes any sense!" she said.

"What were you expecting?" Victoria asked. "It's a first draft, after all. I'm guessing it's full of off-topic rambling, but it probably has a few promising ideas somewhere in there."

"Chaos in the first draft is good," Jon said. "That means the student is striving to write beyond the obvious. When I see a perfectly organized first draft, I'm always skeptical. That's a student who needs to do more thinking and take more risks."

"Jack can't afford to write like Poky, worrying so much about each precious word that he never writes out more than a couple ideas," Phil said. "He has to write like Speedy. If Jack types out enough about those adjectives and memories, he'll find a good concept eventually."

Speedy crumpled up another completed page and threw it down toward Michelle's feet.

"Got it," Michelle said. "First focus on quantity, and then quality will follow. Let's move on." Michelle gave the gate a shove. It didn't budge. She shoved again. Still no movement. The three College Fates looked on in silence. "Hey, how do I open this thing?" Michelle stopped pushing on the gate long enough to turn toward the three College Fates. "I'm not going all the way back down all those stairs." She gave the gate a sharp kick. "Ow!" she cried out.

"You should probably stop kicking things," Jon said. Michelle glared silently in response. "Why don't you try over there?" Jon said, nodding toward the typewriter in the alcove. Michelle walked over and placed her hands above the keys. "Go ahead!"

"Go ahead and what?" Michelle asked.

"Start writing out those adjectives and memories," Victoria said.

"Just like that?" Michelle asked. "I don't feel very inspired right now."

Jon smiled. "Start typing, and the inspiration will follow!" Jon said.

Michelle clacked away on the typewriter for a few seconds and then stopped. The numeral 3 appeared on the scoreboard in the alcove above the typewriter.

"Three words per minute?" Jon asked. "You're never going to open the gate with that kind of score."

"Give her some time to warm up," Victoria said. "She'll get it." Sure enough, Michelle's fingers began to fly across the keyboard at a faster pace, and the number on the scoreboard increased from 3 to 22 to 47 words per minute. *Clack-clack-clackety-clack.* When the scoreboard hit 50, a buzzer sounded, echoing off the Monkey Gate and the metallic walls below. The Monkey Gate slowly creaked open.

"You did it!" Phil said. "Remember to tell Jack that the first draft is all about writing as much as possible as fast as possible. Here, take this to remind you." Phil handed Michelle a small plush monkey dressed in a green jacket and a green fez. "Your own souvenir Speedy."

"Thank you! Now what?" Michelle asked, taking the monkey from Phil and placing it in her tote bag. "I can tell Jack to write fast and to write a lot. But I'm not sure where to go from there."

"Shall we?" Victoria gestured toward the open Monkey Gate. The group filed through to where the Stairway widened enough to let Michelle and the three College Fates walk side by side.

Finding Flaws and Obstacles

"We call this section of the Stairway the Gallery," Phil said. "No stairs here, so we'll get a bit of a breather." The Gallery extended 100 yards in front of the group. Walls painted white rose up from the wooden floor to a height of 12 feet. Unlike the other portions of the Stairway, the Gallery had a ceiling and was fully enclosed. The ceiling, painted white like the walls, anchored a track lighting system which illuminated more portraits. The portraits were all 18 inches by 24 inches, hung vertically, and set in black metal frames with white matte. Instrumental jazz played softly in the background.

Michelle walked over to the first picture on the wall to the left. "That's Jack!" she said, pointing to the picture of a smiling teenage boy dressed in a black tuxedo. "I remember taking that picture at my sister's wedding two years ago."

"They're all of Jack," Victoria said, sweeping her arm forward toward the far end of the Gallery as the group continued walking past pictures. "This is a place for you to continue contemplating what the most important thing is for colleges to know about him."

"After Jack has written out his fast first draft the way you did at the Monkey Gate, you'll ask him about his main point," Phil said. "You can think of it as a thesis sentence."

As the group proceeded through the Gallery, Michelle stopped for a few seconds to study each portrait in silence. After viewing the 50th smiling portrait of Jack, Michelle interrupted the silence. "Something's not right here," she said.

"Is one of the pictures not of Jack?" Jon asked. "I'm supposed to change the pictures for each new parent who walks through the Gallery, but sometimes I miss one."

"No, they're all of Jack," Michelle said. "It's not that. It's that these pictures are all just so… perfect. That's what's wrong. They're too perfect!" Michelle took a step closer to the wall so that her face was just three inches away from the portrait she was examining. Michelle walked back to the previous portrait, looking at it closely, and then turned toward the three College Fates. "I knew it. Jack has a small scar on the outer edge of his right eyebrow from when he and his classmate bumped heads in third grade. Lots of blood and five stitches. But in these photos the scar is gone. These pictures have been touched up. Like they are just showing his good side. It's not the real Jack!"

"That's what we call the 'airbrushed portrait problem,'" Jon said. "It happens whenever the student writes an essay that makes him seem impossibly perfect."

"Seventeen years of studying, sports, and service are leading up to college applications, so it's not surprising parents and students want to impress the colleges," Phil said. "Many students try to impress by writing something lofty that portrays them in an exalted fashion, as if colleges wouldn't want to know who they really are. The result is an 'airbrushed portrait,' which shows the student as perfect but unrelatable."

"I get not going overboard with trying to be impressive," Michelle said. "I would never want Jack to lie about what he's done. That's not how we raised him. But achievements, like winning Mock Trial competitions, are part of his experience. Are you saying that Jack's Main Essay should skip talking about achievements?"

"The applications give Jack plenty of space to describe his achievements," Victoria said. "He has the Activities Section, the Honors and Awards Section, and the Additional Information Section. Even if the Main Essay doesn't cover all his achievements, the application will."

"The Main Essay often does touch on achievements," Jon said, "but it should offer new information that isn't covered in the other sections of the application."

"When it comes to the Main Essay, yes, the starting thesis for many students is something like, 'Look what I achieved,' or 'Look what I learned,'"

Phil said. "The student has done or learned something meaningful, and he wants the Main Essay to show that."

"The problem is that overemphasizing achievement can make the student blend in instead of stand out," Victoria said. "Applicants with Hooks relating to exceptional achievements might be fine, but for most students, emphasizing achievement is a missed chance to come across as a relatable person. Suppose a student writes about accomplishing X, Y, and Z as the president of a school club. But you have tens of thousands of other students writing the same thing."

"Then how do I help Jack come up with a thesis that helps him stand out?" Michelle asked.

"Instead of settling for a 'look-what-I-achieved' thesis, go for a 'look-what-I-achieved-in-spite-of-this-flaw-or-obstacle' thesis," Jon said. "That way, Jack can impress the reader by writing about an important achievement or lesson, and he can relate to the reader by writing about what he overcame."

The group passed by a picture of Jack smiling and holding a certificate indicating he had volunteered for over 100 hours. "You can also help Jack make the achievement or lesson learned in his thesis more precise by asking the good old 'Five Ws': Who, What, Where, When, and Why," Jon said, pointing to the picture of Jack with the certificate. "For example, if Jack ends up writing a thesis about community service teaching him compassion, you can push for more detail. Compassionate to whom, exactly? In what circumstances? Where were you? When did you show this compassion? Why is compassion critical to understanding who you are or what you hope to do?"

"I don't know if he'll have answers for any of these questions," Michelle said.

"Most students don't, at least not right away," Victoria said. "He'll need to do some more talking and writing to figure it all out, but anything Jack can do to add detail is worth the effort because it shows his self-awareness."

"Maybe it's easier if we show you in the rest of the Gallery what we mean," Phil said, motioning to the rest of the group to keep walking. "Take a look." The identically sized, framed, and spaced pictures of Jack gave way to a hodgepodge of photographs of different sizes mounted on the walls at random intervals. "Remember this one?" Phil asked, pointing to a shot of Jack scowling in the driver's seat of the family car.

"We were exiting the parking structure, and I told Jack he was too close to the gate arm, but he kept saying, 'It's fine, Mom, it's fine,'" Michelle said. "He kept saying that right until the gate crashed into the hood. There was no parking attendant, and of course this was the only lane out. The drivers behind us were furious, and it took us 20 minutes to get it all sorted out."

"I'm not sure this exact memory is the way to go for Jack's Main Essay," Victoria said, "but writing about the flaw of being stubborn might be a good way to show personal growth."

"Really?" Michelle asked. "Caring and curious I can see, but stubborn sounds too negative."

"We don't want Jack to come off like a jerk," Jon said. "At the same time, if we can show Jack as a real person who is working on his flaws, that shows his maturity. For example, he could talk about how he would handle the situation differently next time."

"Flaws can be great starting points for drafts, especially for privileged kids who have not faced much adversity in their lives," Victoria said. "Better to write about a flaw than to try to over-dramatize a comfortable upbringing. Not everyone faces obstacles, but everyone has character flaws. That's why flawed characters are more relatable and fun to read about."

"One of my students — a super-nice kid — kept writing drafts about how important it was to him to make others feel welcome," Jon said. "It all started because he used to be shy and kind of a loner. The problem was his essay showed him as this perfect, nice person. It was just boring."

"What did you tell him?" Michelle asked.

"I told him to be real, not perfect," Jon said. "He kept writing, and eventually he confessed that his competitive nature sometimes made it hard to be nice. When he was playing basketball with his best friend, he had talked trash and knocked him over. Then he talked about how he tried to work on this flaw."

"Writing about flaws is one way to be a real person," Phil said. "Writing about obstacles is another." Phil pointed to a snapshot on the right that showed Jack asleep at a kitchen table littered with math books and scratch paper covered with formulas and numbers. "When's that picture from?"

"Jack's sophomore year," Michelle said. "After that car accident I told you about, Jack really stepped up with family responsibilities, especially in helping out with his little sister, Hannah. By the time he could finally start his homework, it was usually after 10:00 pm, and he was exhausted. For three months straight, he would end up falling asleep at the kitchen table, and I would wake him up and make him a snack so he could finish. But he managed to keep his grades up. That's the good part of his stubborn side, I guess."

"That obstacle is a great possibility for the Main Essay," Victoria said. "Writing about flaws or obstacles might seem risky, but it's even riskier to write an airbrushed portrait, one that looks perfect and accomplished without a hint of flaws or obstacles that might make the student relatable to the reader."

"I tell my students, 'If colleges reject you, at least let them reject the real you,'" Jon said. "An airbrushed portrait is a fake portrait, and it will look just like the portraits of all the other students who are trying to impress the colleges by pretending to be perfect."

"No matter what adjectives or memories Jack writes about, he has to come across as a real person," Phil said as the group approached the door at the far end of the Gallery. "Especially for high-achievers, it's counter-intuitive to write about shortcomings and challenges."

"The more Jack writes, the faster he'll figure out a thesis that touches not only on achievements or lessons learned, but on the flaws or conflicts he encountered along the way," Victoria said. "That's how you resolve the airbrushed portrait problem." Victoria opened the door so that the group could exit the Gallery, and Michelle and the three College Fates made their way outside.

As the door from the Gallery slammed shut behind them, Michelle looked up at the next section of the Stairway, which had high brick walls on both sides. The group stood in the shadows, but small patches of sunlight dotted the stairs above. "This is one of Victoria's favorite parts of the Stairway," Jon said as the group began to climb the stairs. "The murals you see on the walls are based on the various circles of Dante's *Inferno*."

"One of my students shared my love for art history, and she's a talented artist, so I asked her if she'd be willing to take on a project that illustrates the misery of the writing process," Victoria said.

"I think she captured the agony," Michelle said, pointing to a scene depicting students being tossed about in a whirlwind. "But what's with all these holes?" Michelle pointed to one of dozens of basketball-sized holes that perforated the wall. "It looks like someone took a giant sledgehammer to the walls."

Fixing the Invisible Essay

"That was last year," Jon said. "We never should have taken that dad up on the Stairway. It was December, way too late in the season, but we felt bad because he was absolutely clueless about how to help his daughter with the Main Essay. He knew it, too. The Boss had hired a contractor to demolish and rebuild a small section of the wall, and the contractor left his sledgehammer out one day. The dad was so stressed by the time he got here that he grabbed that sledgehammer and went to town. We still haven't found the funds to fix the holes yet."

"In the meantime, we've made the holes part of our presentation about the Main Essay," Phil said. "It turns out they illustrate another writing problem many students face."

"Which is what?" Michelle asked as she approached one of the holes and peered through.

"Many important details from the mural are gone," Jon said. "Completely missing. It's the same thing with first drafts of the Main Essay. They're missing the details needed to present a complete picture."

"We call this the 'invisible portrait problem,'" Victoria said. "For a Main Essay to let colleges get to know Jack, it has to create mental pictures. That means the reader has to be able to imagine Jack in action and in conversation."

"Most of us aren't used to talking in a way that creates mental pictures," Phil said. "Think of how you describe a new acquaintance to friends. You might use words like funny, nice, or sweet. These words get the general idea across, but they don't create a mental picture."

"But what about the Walls of Adjectives?" Michelle asked. "They're full of invisible words."

"Adjectives are a convenient starting point, but the sights, sounds, and other sensory details from your memories will form the mental pictures that help the colleges really see and know Jack," Victoria said.

"When I'm sitting down with a student to discuss a first draft, I always start by asking for more details about what the student saw, did, said, or heard," Jon said. "Anything Jack saw or anything Jack did is something the reader will be able to imagine seeing, and anything Jack said or heard is part of a conversation the reader will be able to imagine hearing."

"Really, any detail that hits one of the five senses is useful," Victoria said. "Sights, sounds, smells, tastes, and textures all help colleges understand what Jack's like and what he can bring to campus. That's what we mean by sensory details."

"I do want colleges to see Jack clearly," Michelle said, "but how does it work, exactly? How do you turn an invisible portrait into something readers can see?"

"One of my students wrote a couple sentences in a first draft about how she crocheted gifts to cheer up her friends," Jon said. "It was a start, but it was invisible because I didn't know what she had made. After some discussion, she mentioned she once crocheted a piece of poop for her friend as a joke. Now I had a mental picture! No reader would forget a crocheted piece of poop. It was a visible image that captured her sense of humor."

Michelle and the three College Fates continued plodding up the stairs.

"Here's another example," Phil said. "I had a student who wanted to write about his leadership in the YMCA's Youth and Government program. He wrote in a first draft that one responsibility he took on was mentoring other students. He was clearly doing something useful, but I couldn't visualize it. After I pushed him, he mentioned he spent a lot of time working with other participants to help them improve their speaking skills. For his next draft, he wrote about specific conversations he had while working one-on-one with three other students. Those conversations put the reader in the room with him, and they highlighted his patience and passion."

"When you talk about adding sights and sounds to create a mental picture, it seems so easy," Michelle said. "It's the old 'show, don't tell' advice. But if it's really that easy, why don't more students write this way?"

"Most kids have never written a personal essay before, so they don't understand that sights and sounds are crucial to making a personal essay personal," Victoria said. "Some who do know about sights and sounds don't want to put in the effort. It only takes a few words and a few seconds to write an invisible summary like 'I mentored younger students.' It could take an hour and 500 words to write about the conversations where that mentoring occurred."

"But the details about conversations with other Youth and Government students, really?" Michelle asked. "That seems so trivial. I was hoping for something grander."

"That's exactly what our students say," Phil said. "They want to start with the grand stuff, not the mundane sights and sounds. But if Jack skips the sights and sounds, he's skipping personal details that help the reader imagine what it's like to hang out with him, to be in the same room with him, to know him. He'll end up painting an invisible portrait." Phil pointed to a hole in the wall to the right. "He'll just disappear."

"But I can solve the invisible portrait problem by asking Jack to write about more sights, sounds, and sensory details?" Michelle asked.

"You got it," Jon said. "Second, third, and fourth drafts are all about expanding on what's already there, and you can never go wrong by asking Jack to write out details that will create a mental picture for the reader."

Michelle and the three College Fates reached the end of the mural section of the Stairway and stepped up onto a circular landing.

Cleaning Up the Messy Essay

An easel with a portrait of Jack, hair down to his shoulders, stood in front of them. Behind the easel, an overgrown shrub sprouted six feet tall from a planter at the center of the landing.

"I see you let Jack grow his hair out," Phil said.

"He promised to cut it before graduation," Michelle said, "and I have to choose my battles. I'd prefer a clean-cut look, but he wants shaggy, so that's how it goes, at least for now."

"A shaggy portrait," Jon said. "That's a problem students face with the Main Essay, too."

"What do you mean?" Michelle asked.

"Let's say Jack solves the airbrushed portrait problem by mentioning flaws or obstacles, not just achievements," Jon said. "For Jack, that might mean talking about why it was hard for him to show his compassion. Let's also say Jack solves the invisible portrait problem by adding plenty of sights, sounds, and other sensory details. That means talking about specific moments where someone observing Jack would think, 'Compassion!' By writing as much as possible as fast as possible, Jack will have a draft of hundreds, maybe thousands, of words, but it will be wild and messy. That's the 'shaggy portrait problem.'"

"I could definitely see this happening to Jack," Michelle said. "He'll write out all the details he can think of about his compassionate side, but then we'll have to figure out how to trim it down."

"There are five steps," Phil said. "But it's easier if we show you while we tell you." Phil pulled out four small pairs of garden shears, handing one each to Michelle, Victoria, and Jon, and keeping one for himself. "Let's head over to that bush over there." The group walked past the easel with the picture of Jack in all his shaggy teenage glory and then over to the shrub in the middle of the landing.

"The first step to trimming the Main Essay is to chop off the parts you don't need," Jon said as he began to cut a few inches off the shrub's longest branches. "For Jack, that might mean deleting any sentences or paragraphs from his rough draft that don't relate to compassion."

"You and Jack can highlight all the parts of his draft that demonstrate his compassion and cut and paste them into a new draft," Victoria said.

"Anything that doesn't relate to Jack's compassion you can leave behind," Phil said. "Why don't you start cutting?" Phil asked Michelle as he pointed to a long branch that was shooting out horizontally from the shrub.

"The second step is to open the essay by putting the reader in the middle of the action, also known as *in medias res*," Victoria said.

"Let's trim the shrub so there's a big sphere toward the base," Jon said. Michelle and the three College Fates continued to work their shears with vigor.

"I tell my students that the intro is a great place to give the reader a conflict or a mystery," Victoria says. "That draws the reader in."

"That sounds complicated," Michelle said.

"It's not as bad as you think," Jon said. "Jack can think back to a particular moment when he showed compassion. Then he can open the essay with action or dialogue from that moment."

"Most students want to add a bunch of background information," Phil said. "Colleges don't need to know the details of Jack's elementary or middle school career. For most students, it makes sense to start the essay with a critical moment from high school."

"The third step is to give context to the conflict or mystery, which helps explain it," Victoria said.

"Giving context is the function of the body paragraphs," Jon said. "Let's trim a smaller sphere over the first one." The group continued to trim the shrub.

"You want to make sure that each body paragraph communicates unique information," Phil said. "For example, if Jack ends up writing something about compassion, he might find that one good anecdote about his sister, Hannah, is enough. Three anecdotes about her might be redundant."

"Giving context might mean that Jack explains how he showed compassion in other circumstances," Jon said. "Maybe the paragraph about compassion toward Hannah is followed by one about compassion toward his classmates or toward others in his community. The idea is for each body paragraph to show a different dimension of the same one important thing — in Jack's case, compassion."

"The fourth step is to resolve the conflict or mystery and show the impact of the experience," Victoria said.

"A simple way to do that is to save the thesis for the conclusion," Jon said. "Saving the explanation of why all the details matter and what they all mean is an easy way to end the essay with a fresh insight. Let's trim one more sphere above the other two."

"Hold on," Michelle said as she stopped cutting. "I thought essays should start with the thesis so the reader knows the main point."

"For analytical essays, like for English or history class, yes," Phil said. "For personal essays like this, no. Remember what Victoria said about creating a mystery in the intro? If Jack puts the thesis in the intro it will be a spoiler that kills all the suspense."

"Imagine Jack starts his essay with a conversation with you after you broke your leg," Jon said. "Maybe it's one where he is reluctant to take on more responsibility. Then the essay continues with an anecdote about helping take care of Hannah. And Jack develops this idea of compassion further by talking about how he made sacrifices to be there for his friends. The reader will see from these details that Jack is compassionate. But then Jack can explain why compassion matters to him, maybe on a personal level, or maybe in terms of what major or career he wants to pursue. Spelling it out at the end leaves the reader thinking, 'It all makes perfect sense now.'"

"The fifth and final step to trimming the Main Essay is to print it out and read it aloud," Victoria said. "Words look different on the printed page than they do on the computer screen."

"Reading aloud is an easy way to catch stray words, awkward sentences, and grammatical errors," Jon said. "When you've read a draft 20 times on a screen, it's easy to miss a typo. Let's do one final pass on this shrub for any branches or leaves that are poking out. We want this to be shaped perfectly." Michelle and the three College Fates continued snipping, an inch here, an inch there.

"You want to make sure Jack's essay sounds like Jack," Victoria said. "If he reads it aloud and it sounds like words he would actually say, that's a good sign."

"What about word choice?" Michelle asked. "I want his essay to sound sophisticated."

"That's probably the hardest thing for parents to let go of," Phil said. "I'm not saying word choice doesn't matter. We don't need an essay littered with dead words like 'things' or lazy verbs like 'have.' But we don't want an essay full of thesaurus words, either.

"The ocean can be blue," Jon said. "It doesn't have to be cerulean."

"Parents put too much emphasis on word choice," Phil said. "Beautiful words can't save an essay that lacks a compelling thesis or memorable supporting details."

"But there have to be times when it's OK to change the words, right?" Michelle asked. "Or no, never?"

"Confusing sentences should be revised, grammatical errors should be corrected, and redundancies should be eliminated," Victoria said. "But if the issue is that you want to say something your way and Jack wants to say something his way, let him say it his way. It's his essay, after all!"

"That does it for the five steps to trim the Main Essay," Jon said. "Phil, do you still have those tennis balls from our match this morning?"

Phil rummaged around in his robes and took out two white tennis balls. "Here you go," Phil said, handing them to Jon.

"It's not a snowman if it doesn't have eyes," Jon said. "Well, it's not a snowman, anyway, but you know what I mean." Jon turned toward Michelle. "Which way should the eyes face? Out toward Fall Hell?"

"Toward the top of the Stairway," Michelle said without hesitation. "Eyes on the prize."

"That's the spirit!" Victoria said.

As Jon walked to the other side of the topiary to place the tennis ball eyes, Phil handed Michelle an envelope. "Here, we want you to have this," he said.

"What is it?" Michelle asked as she began to open the envelope.

"We know it will take a lot of effort to help Jack develop a high-resolution Main Essay that shows what a great kid he is," Phil said, "so we wanted to leave you with a little inspiration."

Michelle removed a photograph from the envelope and smiled. "Oh, this is one of my favorite pictures of Jack! I was inside because my broken leg hadn't healed yet, but Jack and Hannah were outside throwing snowballs at each other. He threw one that accidentally hit her in the face, and she started to cry. He tried to hug her, but she said the only way she would be happy again was if he made her a special snowman, so he spent 30 minutes working on it. He put two branches coming out of the head like horns and told her this was a reindeer snowman. This is a picture of them laughing together in front of it. I wanted to open the door and say something, but it was one of those magic childhood moments, and I didn't want to break the spell. I don't think I ever showed him this picture. That's my Jack, though. Always making sure everyone around him is happy."

"That's the kind of portrait we want to show the colleges through the Main Essay," Jon said. "A vivid image of who he is and what matters to him."

"You can help colleges see a true portrait of Jack," Victoria said. "Getting from brainstorming to final draft of the Main Essay takes time and effort, nothing more."

"Of course, there's uncertainty along the way," Jon said, "because especially in the early stages, you'll be wondering whether Jack will find a way to elevate his essay beyond the usual clichés."

"If he sticks with it, he can do it," Phil said. "Look at the sign!" Phil pointed to another sign welded to the far side of the landing. "Just 242 steps to College Heaven!"

Words of Wisdom from the Boss

"Your child does not have to be a good writer to write a good Main Essay. A successful Main Essay helps the colleges see your child as a real person. Beyond mentioning accomplishments or lessons learned, the Main Essay should touch on flaws or obstacles your child has overcome, and it should include sights, sounds, and other sensory details. Writing all this out happens over the course of days or weeks, not hours, so encourage your child to start early and to write as many words as possible as quickly as possible. Writing is a chaotic process, so remind your child that uncertainty about what to say and how to say it is normal."

As the small group continued its ascent, the surface of the stairs became pitted and cracked. Grime and dust had worked its way into all the imperfections and depressions. The height of the steps doubled from six inches to twelve, and after a minute, the only sounds from Michelle and the three College Fates were those of labored breathing.

Michelle stopped walking and wrapped her hands behind her head to catch her breath. "Why are the stairs so dirty up here?" Michelle asked. "And why are they so freaking tall?"

"We've come to the Supplemental Essays," Victoria said. "Definitely the worst part of the application process."

"But we're close to the top, right?" Michelle asked. "Didn't that sign say we had just 242 steps to go?"

"Sure, we don't have many left, but they're the steepest steps on the Stairway," Jon said.

"Some students and parents don't appreciate how much work these Supplemental Essays are," Jon said. "We're easily talking ten more essays of 150 to 650 words, though most tend to be 250 to 300."

"Imagine writing this great Main Essay and thinking you're almost done, only to find out that you have ten more essays to write," Victoria said. "Kind of demoralizing."

"I know the feeling," Michelle said, gazing up at the steps above. "But can't we just skip the Supplemental Essays?" Michelle asked. "You did say not all the colleges require them, right?"

"Sure, if you wanted to, you could find colleges that require only the Main Essay but no Supplemental Essays," Victoria said.

"But is that really how you want to build Jack's College List?" Phil asked. "I mean, the list should reflect schools that are good matches for Jack, not schools that are the easiest to apply to."

"Though if it's mid-November and Jack hasn't submitted any applications, sometimes you have to be practical," Jon said. "Hopefully it won't happen to Jack, but if it does, you can start with the Target and Safety Schools that don't ask for Supplemental Essays. At least that way, he's getting some applications in early."

"Can we rest for a few more minutes?" Michelle asked. She paused, placed her left hand on the iron railing, and drew in a deep breath. "I don't know if I can handle more right now."

From the lower reaches of the Stairway, Draggin let out a series of loud roars. The three College Fates turned to stare at Michelle in silence.

"OK, OK!" Michelle said. "I know already. Draggin is coming. Stop procrastinating, keep moving, blah blah blah."

"Like I tell my students, you might not have much energy now, but you're definitely not going to have more energy later," Jon said.

Michelle resumed her climb with a speed and enthusiasm which could charitably be called trudging, gripping the railing as she went. "What are these Supplemental Essays?" Michelle asked. "You might as well tell me."

"There are four kinds you should know about," Jon said. "The Why This College Essay, the Community Essay, the Activity Essay, and the University of California Personal Insight Questions."

"Before Jack starts working on the Supplemental Essays for any application, you'll want to sit down with him and read all the essay prompts," Phil said. "Don't let him start writing until he has read all of them."

"What difference does that make?" Michelle asked, still resting her hand on the railing.

"It's important to think about the different sides of Jack's personality and experiences that you want to show the colleges," Jon said. "The Main Essay covers the most important thing about Jack. If a college requires two

Supplemental Essays, you want to make sure those essays cover the second and third most important things about Jack."

"Plus, you want to make sure Jack isn't repeating himself in the Supplemental Essays," Victoria said. "Each Supplemental Essay should provide new material, not repeat what's in the Main Essay or in any other Supplemental Essay." Victoria paused. "Oh, and you might want to keep your hands off the railing for the next little bit. Bird droppings from Romeo."

"Ew, gross," Michelle said, removing her hand from the railing. "But who's Romeo?"

From above, the climbers heard the call of a bird that sounded as if it were being strangled in a most unpleasant fashion. *Squawk! Squawk! Squawk!* The cries grew louder as the bird came into view.

The Why This College Essay

"Hi, Romeo," Jon said as the bird flew closer.

"So Romeo is just a parrot?" Michelle asked.

"A macaw, from what I can tell," Jon said. Romeo landed on the railing next to Michelle. He was about three feet long from his beak to the tip of his tail, with yellow feathers on his breast and blue feathers on his back and wings. "He's here to help parents understand the Why This College Essay."

"Say you love me!" Romeo said. "Say you love me! Say you love me! Say you love me!"

Michelle furrowed her brow and looked from Romeo over to the three College Fates. "Is this some kind of riddle?" Michelle asked. "What does 'Say you love me!' have to do with the Why This College Essay?"

"Colleges want to know they're not wasting an offer of admission on students who don't know them or understand them," Victoria said. "The Why This College Essay explains why the college is a good fit for the student and vice-versa."

"That means explaining why Jack is a good academic fit," Phil said. "Academics are the heart of this essay. It's great when a student loves the campus or the football or the Greek life, but the response to this essay can't avoid talking about what the student might want to study."

"That's almost impossible!" Michelle said. "Jack's only 17! He's not sure yet what he wants to study. How can he write an essay about how much he loves a major?"

"Victoria might not be the right person to ask about that," Phil said. "I mean, she's the one who told her husband she loved him on just her first date."

"Third date," Victoria said.

"Whatever," Jon said.

"But how can Jack write about loving a college he barely knows?" Michelle asked. "This is supposed to be a long-term relationship, not some summer fling."

"It is ridiculous," Phil agreed. "But we have to play the game."

"And play it well," Victoria said. "It's one thing to tell a college, 'I'm interested in you because you have all these great qualities,' and it's another to say, 'I'm in love with you — I have to be with you.' We're going for an essay that says, 'I have to be with you.'"

"The colleges want to be wanted," Jon said. "If they're going to offer Jack a spot, they have to believe there's a reasonable chance he'll enroll."

"Squawk, squawk, squawk!" Romeo shrieked. "Say you love me! Say you love me! Say you love me!"

"That's super-freaking-annoying," Michelle said. "Is there any way to shut that thing up?"

"I wonder where Draggin is," Phil said. "Maybe she's still hungry."

"Just tell me how to do the Why This College Essay, and let's keep climbing while we're at it," Michelle said. "I don't even know where to begin."

"First off, as Phil said, this question is mostly about academics," Jon said. "Campus traditions and the football games are great, but our first goal is to show the university why Jack is a good academic fit."

"Many students like to write about how beautiful a campus is," Phil said. "One of my students wrote a response that could have been inspired by Thoreau's *Walden*. After a visit, she wrote about seeing an expansive lush green lawn with beautiful trees and the scent of the nearby ocean. I told her she was going to the college to study, not to vacation. In her next draft, she added that the beautiful trees provided the perfect shade under which she could envision herself studying and doing yoga."

"But I told you," Michelle said. "Jack doesn't even know what he wants to study. How can he talk about academic fit?"

"It doesn't have to be super-specific," Victoria said. "It could be as simple as biology, political science, or business."

"Many of my students have no idea what they want to study," Phil said. "But what can we do? We're not going to pretend, but we do need to find something plausible."

"How are we supposed to do that?" Michelle said.

"Say you love me! Say you love me! Say you love me!" Romeo cried.

"Start with Jack's classes," Jon said. "Any favorites? Any research projects where he had to do some extra exploring? Those are some possibilities."

"Another is Jack's activities. Which academic areas might they relate to?" Phil asked. "A kid doing Debate Club might be interested in international relations. A football player might want to study biology to better understand concussions. It's much easier to write the Why This College Essay when you have a specific major in mind."

"What if he's just not sure about his major?" Michelle asked. "Jack might do business, or he might do computer science."

"That's something to keep in mind when you're working on the College List," Victoria said. "You'll want to make sure the list includes Reach, Target, and Safety Schools for both areas of interest. If Jack ends up choosing computer science, it won't help much to apply to Safety Schools that only offer business."

"No matter what major Jack writes about, he can open the Why This College Essay with a 'this-is-where-it-all-began' moment," Jon said. "I'm talking about a particular experience Jack could point to and say, 'This is where my academic interest began.' It could be a book he read about entrepreneurship, or it might be a mobile app he programmed on his own."

Romeo continued to squawk. Michelle could barely hear the wise words of the three College Fates above the din. Slowly, with a scowl on her face, Michelle edged closer toward the railing upon which Romeo had perched.

"After you and Jack find that anecdote about what experience sparked his academic interest, you can identify details from the college's website that show how he would pursue that interest," Phil said.

"You might have to actually sit there and click through the website with him," Jon said. "I can't tell you how many times students swear, 'I couldn't find anything,' and then we sit down together and find five details within a couple minutes. Digital natives, ha!"

"Look for upper-division courses that sound interesting," Phil said. "Then look at the professors' biographies and papers."

"See if there's anyone doing research in an area that might interest Jack," Victoria said. "Ask what other research programs, internships, or student organizations would let Jack explore his interest."

"Isn't this kind of impersonal?" Michelle said. "I can't imagine any college being impressed by an essay that recites facts from a website."

"Squawk, squawk!" Romeo cried. "Say you love me! Say you love me!"

Michelle was now standing two feet away from Romeo. Even as the three College Fates droned on about the Why This College Essay, she kept her eyes fixed on the blue bird.

"Well, there are limits," Phil said. "I told one student working on this prompt to go to the college website and learn some things that fit in with what he was interested in studying. In the next draft I saw lines such as '260 degree programs,' 'faculty includes Pulitzer Prizewinners and MacArthur Fellows,' and 'award-winning program educates tomorrow's medical professionals.' I said it sounded like he was writing a brochure for the college. He said he did what I told him and got the information from the college website. I said, 'Wait, did you pull direct quotes from the website?' To which he unapologetically said, 'Yes.'"

"Pretty lazy," Michelle said.

"Right," Jon said. "You can't just recite facts about the school. That's impersonal, for sure. You also have to say why the facts matter. Usually why the facts matter is because they further some interest or career goal the student has. And if the student really cannot find any reason the opportunities matter, maybe the college isn't a good match."

"Or maybe the college has a bad website!" Victoria said. "Another problem with just reciting facts, though, is plagiarism," Victoria added. "You won't win any points for copying text from the website and using it without attribution."

"That's why you start this essay with an anecdote about your child's academic interests," Jon said. "When you mention all the opportunities inside and outside the classroom that might appeal to your child, you're not just saying, 'This would be a great opportunity.' You're also saying why."

"The Why This College Essay is a bridge between your child's past and his future," Victoria said.

"You're arguing that based on what Jack has already done and has already shown an interest in, this particular college would be the perfect place for him to continue exploring," Phil said.

"That's what fit is," Jon said.

"Say you love me!" Romeo shrieked. "Say you love me! Say you love me!"

Michelle clenched and then relaxed her fists.

"So the first part of the Why This College Essay is an anecdote about Jack's academic interest," Michelle said. "And the second part is a mention of some courses and opportunities at the school that would further Jack's academic interest. Anything else he needs to add?"

"Buzzwords," Jon said.

"Also known as core values," Victoria said.

"Or contacts with the school," Phil said.

"Say you love me!" Romeo called out again, for what seemed like the 100th time in three minutes.

"Seriously? Does this bird say any other words?" Michelle asked.

"Say you love me!" Romeo answered. "Say you love me!"

"We're almost done with the Why This College Essay," Phil said. "He'll be on his way soon."

"You can figure out a college's core values by looking at the language on its website," Jon said. "Try looking for the About Us section or the mission statement."

"For example, Jesuit schools will always mention social justice and being a person for God and others," Phil said.

"Use common sense," Victoria said. "If the website mentions a value such as collaboration 15 times, then Jack should try to work 'collaboration' into the anecdote, the college's opportunities, and the conclusion," Victoria said.

"Say you love me!" Romeo called out again.

Michelle clenched her fists again. "Quiet!" she yelled. "Stop saying that!"

"Take a deep breath," Jon said.

"Don't tell me what to do!" Michelle snapped.

"Don't let Romeo distract you," Victoria said. "We have to deal with him. Remember all those reps you met at the College Fair and all that great info you learned from Barbie and Ken? This is the place to mention those conversations."

"Say you love me! Say you love me! Say you love me!" Romeo would not relent.

"There are just three steps to the Why This College Essay," Phil said.

"Say you love me!" Romeo squawked.

"First, an anecdote about an academic interest," Victoria said.

"Second, details about opportunities the college offers," Jon said.

"Third, buzzwords, core values, and conversations with people from the school to show you really understand the spirit of the school," Victoria said.

"Say you love me!" Romeo said.

"That's really all there is to it," Phil said.

"Say you love me! Say you love —" Before Romeo could utter his inane plea one more time, Michelle reached over and swatted him, sending a flurry of blue feathers into the air. Romeo let out an even louder squawk, and he left a pile of bird droppings all over Michelle's new shoes as he flew away from the Stairway.

"Stupid bird!" Michelle yelled out.

"Squawk! Squawk!" Romeo called out as he alighted on the railing several yards below. "Your kid's not getting in! Your kid's not getting in! Your kid's not getting in! Ha ha ha ha ha ha!"

With that, Michelle reached down, removed her right shoe and hurled it at Romeo, hitting him with a glancing blow to the head. The chances of this happening were about as high as an unhooked kid getting into Yale. Romeo squawked and took off from his perch on the railing.

"Woohoo!" Michelle said, lifting her arms in celebration.

Jon turned to Victoria and Phil and lowered his voice. "There's something about this journey to college that really messes with parents' heads. Let's get her to the top of the Stairway ASAP."

"I got this," Victoria said. Turning back to Michelle and using her best you're-doing-just-fine voice, the kind she usually reserved for conversing with recalcitrant young children, Victoria addressed Michelle. "Hey there, how's it going?" She patted Michelle gently on the arm. "That was an amazing throw. What do you say we keep moving so we can get up to the top?"

"Sorry you lost your shoe," Phil said to Michelle. "But you got him!"

"Maybe you want to take off your other shoe," Victoria said. "Barefoot running is a great workout. Your calf muscles will look amazing."

Michelle began heading up the stairs again, only to stop short. "Whoa!" she said, her knees buckling, and her hands shooting out to grab the rail. Phil reached out to catch Michelle until she was steady on her feet again. "My head won't stop spinning."

"A little vertigo is normal this high on the Stairway," Jon said. "But we're almost there. Just a few more steps!"

"I need to rest," Michelle said, taking a seat. "Can't you tell me about the other Supplemental Essays while I sit here for a minute?"

Draggin let out another roar from below. "Uh, I think we better speed this up a little," Victoria said.

"Just one more minute, and I'll be ready to go," Michelle said. "Promise."

Draggin breathed out a rod of flame, and smoke rose from her nostrils as she began to lumber up the stairs.

"Fine, your choice," Phil said, eyeing Draggin as she rapidly advanced up the Stairway. "Aside from the Why This College Essay, you have to understand the Community Essay."

"All right. Tell me about that one," Michelle said from where she sat.

The Community Essay

"The Community Essay asks Jack to describe a community he's a part of, along with his contribution to that community or his place in it," Victoria said.

"Take Draggin, for example," Jon said, pointing down the Stairway. "Where does she belong? Is she a reptile? A bird? A dinosaur? A hero? A villain?"

"Each student has lots of flexibility about how to define 'community,'" Phil said.

"Obvious possibilities for community include a school, a club, a church, or a culture," Jon added.

"Think broadly, and keep an open mind!" Victoria said. "Which communities might not be obvious? Those are the interesting ones."

"Right," Jon said. "One of my students taught himself to code, joined an online forum, answered over 2,000 questions from other people there, and became a moderator of that forum. That counts as a community. It doesn't have to be conventional."

"I had a student describe his community as the evening people who shared the floor of the school building where he spent his nights coding: his fellow coders, an advisor, and the custodian," Phil said.

"If this essay is so much simpler than the others, what stops students from doing a good job?" Michelle asked.

"Fatigue," Phil said.

"I get that," Michelle said, turning her head up again toward the Stairway above.

"Energy and motivation are high for the Main Essay because most students write that one first and because they know so many schools will see it," Jon said.

"When students get to the Community Essay and see it's only 250 words, they figure they can just write whatever, and it will be fine," Phil said.

"We always have to remind our students, 'Quantity, then quality,'" Jon said. "No matter how short an essay is, when it comes to the first draft, Jack has to write as much as possible."

"Like Speedy," Phil said, pointing to the stuffed Sir Speedy monkey that was peeking out of Michelle's tote bag. "If that monkey writes enough bad stuff, eventually he'll write some good stuff, too."

"The same details we talked about before matter here, too," Victoria said. "Sights, sounds, smells, tastes, and textures."

"Think if you were writing about your trip up this Stairway to College Heaven," Jon said. "Maybe your community would include your three faithful guides."

"You could start by writing about stuff we've done together, and you could end with a thesis about what this community means to you," Phil said.

"Hopefully something good," Victoria said.

"Depends on how many more stairs we have left to climb," Michelle said.

"Once you understand the Community Essay, you understand the Activity Essay, too," Phil said.

"Let me guess. That one asks the student to talk about an important extracurricular activity?" Michelle said.

The Activity Essay

"Exactly!" Victoria said. "First do the details from a specific scene with specific people doing or saying specific things at a specific point in time," Victoria said. "Then end with a thesis about why the activity matters."

"Yeah, I have to say — and this is true for the Activities Section of the application and for the essays — most students completely miss the 'why-it-matters' part," Jon said.

"What do you mean?" Michelle asked.

"Jack can't just write the facts about what he did," Jon said. "He has to explain why he's writing about those facts. What do they show about who he is or what he values?"

"How long is this Activity Essay, though?" Michelle asked.

"Usually 150 to 250 words," Victoria said. "It's not going to drag on. But it still needs imagery, conversation, and actions. If it doesn't create a mental picture, then it's just general statements that sound like everyone else's."

"Activity Essays tend to sound alike because everyone has the same thesis: 'This activity taught me this lesson,'" Phil said.

"That's why the sights, sounds, and other sensory details that create mental pictures are so important for the Activity Essay," Victoria said. "I once had a student who described how much she used to admire other girls' feet, and loathe her own, because hers had become so mangled from years of figure skating. Eventually she realized that worrying about her foot aesthetics wasn't going to get her to Nationals. The image she painted was highly effective in showing so much about her character and dedication to her sport. She's now at Stanford."

A warm breeze blew the scent of honeysuckle up the Stairway from the hedge maze below. The late afternoon sun sat low in the sky, bathing the three College Fates and Michelle in an orange light. A haze of smoke hung over the horizon.

"Any other essays?" Michelle asked.

"The University of California Personal Insight Questions, also known as the UC Essays," Jon said.

The University of California Personal Insight Questions

"What's different about the UC Essays?" Michelle asked, pausing on the steps, closing her eyes and taking a long, slow breath.

Victoria looked down the Stairway. Draggin had taken off and was now flying upward at a slow but steady pace. Victoria extended her index finger and moved it in a circular motion, as if to say, "Wrap it up!"

Jon gave Victoria a quick thumbs-up. "For the UC Essays, get to the main point as fast as possible," Jon said. "Jack can say what he did, what obstacles he faced, and what impact the experience had on him and the people around him."

"That's it?" Michelle asked.

"Pretty much," Jon said. "The UC Essays are like the essays students are used to writing for English class. Start with a thesis that has the main point about why the topic matters to Jack, and then get to his supporting details. The UC Essays are about clarity, not storytelling. Don't worry about style, either." Glancing down at Michelle's shoeless feet, he said, "I don't think that will be a problem for you."

"What Jon means to say about style is that you don't need an introduction or a conclusion for the UC Essays," Victoria said. "Word choice isn't a big deal, either. Jack just needs to say whatever he needs to say as clearly and concisely as possible."

"Sometimes the hardest part about the UC Essays is figuring out which prompts to answer," Phil said. "There are eight prompts: leadership, creativity, greatest talent, educational opportunity or barrier, significant challenge, favorite subject, contribution to community, and one unique thing about him."

"Jack only needs to write four of those," Jon said. "Don't overthink it. The goal is to figure out which topics would allow Jack to discuss his four most important qualities or experiences."

"What if he can't decide?" Michelle asked.

"It's the same as with every other essay," Victoria said. "If you're discussing a few options and can't tell which one is best, have Jack try to write all of them out. Most of the time, after students try writing out their ideas, it's pretty clear what works and what doesn't."

"That's it for the essays," Jon said. "We've covered all the big ones. The Why This College Essay, the Community Essay, the Activity Essay, and the UC Essays."

"But there's one last trick of the trade with the writing," Victoria said.

"Which one?" Jon asked as he looked at Victoria. "Oh, right!" Jon smiled and jabbed his finger into the air. "I can't believe I forgot!"

"Well… what is it?" Michelle asked.

"They're talking about the Additional Information Section," Phil said.

The Additional Information Section

"This is a free space for Jack to include anything that didn't make it into the rest of the application, like the Activities Section, the Main Essay, or the Supplemental Essays," Victoria said.

"The Common Application, some college supplements on the Coalition Application, and most other application forms offer some variation of the Additional Information Section," Jon said.

"Is it mandatory?" Michelle asked.

"Optional," Phil said, "but why not use it?"

"You want the final application document to show as much of Jack's life as possible," Jon said. "If there are special circumstances, like illness, divorce, or family responsibilities, or if he wants to explain a bad grade, list extra honors and awards, or write a few sentences about why some activity was especially meaningful, this is the place to do it."

"It's like last call," Phil said. "When Jack hits submit, you want that peace of mind from knowing that the application hasn't left out anything important."

"Won't colleges get annoyed, though?" Michelle asked. "I mean, if they wanted that information, it seems like they would have asked for it."

"Let them decide what's important," Victoria said. "I'm not saying Jack has to fill up the whole Additional Information Section. But I'd much rather see him write more and have the colleges decide it's not important than have him write less and never give colleges the chance to see his whole story."

"I tell my students that, yes, the application has a certain structure and certain constraints," Jon said, "but you need to make the application work for you. Use the application in every way you can imagine to advocate your position that you are worth a serious look."

"In all this writing, whether for the Main Essay, the Supplemental Essays, or the Additional Information Section, the student is the topic," Victoria said. "If Jack's writing captures the essentials of who he is, then he has done a good job."

"Ready to take the final steps?" Phil asked Michelle. "Look! There's the last sign!" Phil pointed to what was, indeed, the final sign on the Stairway: 'College Heaven: 3 Steps.'"

....
Words of Wisdom from the Boss
....

"Beyond the Main Essay, most students have to write numerous Supplemental Essays, including the Why This College Essay, the Community Essay, the Activity Essay, and the University of California Personal Insight Questions. Though the Supplemental Essays are usually shorter than the Main Essay, the sheer number of them makes them exhausting. Make sure that each Supplemental Essay shows a different side of your child and does not repeat information from the Main Essay or from any other section of the application. Though not technically a Supplemental Essay, the Additional Information Section is a great place for your child to write out important info that does not fit anywhere else."

....

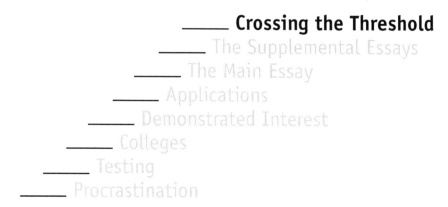

The small group climbed the final three steps into the clouds shrouding the top of the Stairway. "I can't see anything," Michelle said.

"Just a few more seconds!" Victoria said.

Sure enough, the clouds melted away as the group reached the final landing. In front of them stood a shining doorway that bathed them in a warm yellow light. They placed their hands above their eyes to shield against the brightness.

"What happens now?" Michelle asked. "We just walk through?" Before the three College Fates could warn her, Michelle took a step forward. The light intensified, and a surge of heat radiated from the doorway. "And maybe not," Michelle said, jumping back and casting a glance down the Stairway. "Draggin's almost here!" The group could hear the *thunk-thunk-thunk* of her tail against the railing on the stairs just yards below, and it was getting louder. "Why are you just standing there? Do something!"

Draggin reached the final step, pushed past the group to stand in front of the flaming doorway, and turned around to face Michelle and the three College Fates. Draggin opened her mouth, but this time no fire flew out. Instead, she turned to Michelle and spoke. "The journey to College Heaven is full of obstacles," Draggin said. Michelle opened her mouth as if to speak and then closed it without saying a word. "Procrastination, anxiety, ignorance, to name a few," Draggin continued. "When you learn how college applications work, you prepare yourself and your child to overcome these obstacles."

"I thought you were trying to kill us!" Michelle said.

Draggin ignored Michelle and continued with her speech. "Listen carefully. Listen to people who know the ins and outs of the process. Listen to your intuition about what makes sense for Jack. Most of all, listen to what Jack wants. If you listen very hard, the tune will come to you at last." An epic electric guitar solo jumped from hidden speakers out over the Stairway and beyond. Draggin roared and sent a volley of fireballs skyward.

"Were all those pyrotechnics really necessary?" Michelle asked. "And did you really have to chase us this whole time?"

"Sometimes one must light a fire under the nether regions of another to induce productive action," Draggin said. "But you're interrupting. I practiced this speech for a long time. So if you don't mind..."

"My bad," Michelle said, raising her hands in front of her, palms out, in apology.

"Go ahead, Draggin," Jon said.

"No one may enter College Heaven without making the vows," Draggin said. "Are you willing to make the vows, Michelle?"

"I think so," Michelle said. Draggin looked at her in silence. "Yes, I'm willing."

"Very well," Draggin said. "Do you promise to support Jack through the whole college planning process?"

"I do," Michelle said.

"Do you promise not to get caught up in what other parents are saying and doing?" Draggin asked.

"I do," Michelle said.

"Do you promise to help Jack set realistic goals?" Draggin asked.

"I do," Michelle said.

"Do you promise to give Jack all of your patience, support, and love?"

"I do," Michelle said.

"And to give him his favorite snacks?" Draggin said.

"Yes," Michelle said with a smile.

"You have made the vows," Draggin said. "Now do everything in your power to keep them." Michelle nodded. "You may enter College Heaven."

Michelle moved toward the threshold, only to be brushed aside by Victoria.

"Yes! I'm getting nachos!" Victoria cried out as she pumped her fists and rushed past the rest of the group into College Heaven.

"The nachos are good," Jon said to Michelle, "but still, she could have let you go first."

"After you," Phil said to Michelle.

"Wait!" Draggin said. "Before you cross over, I want you to have this." Draggin handed Michelle a scroll tied with a purple ribbon.

"What's this?" Michelle asked.

"Open it and see," Draggin said. Michelle untied the ribbon and unrolled the parchment.

"This is my College Planning Scroll," Draggin said. "Look, I even lightly toasted it to make it seem really ancient, and I did all the calligraphy by hand. Pretty great, right? I give one to every parent who makes it to the top of the Stairway."

Michelle held the unfurled scroll with both hands and gazed upon it with wonder. Her face shone in the light of divine knowledge. "It's so beautiful," she whispered to herself.

"You're ready," Jon said, beckoning toward the doorway. Michelle crossed the threshold and vanished into College Heaven. "It was all worth it," Phil and Jon heard her say from across the other side.

Phil and Jon turned to Draggin. "What about you?" Phil asked. "Will you be joining us?"

"Not today," Draggin said. "The Boss has me working late. I have three more parents to torment and motivate today, plus eight more tomorrow. Fall is a hectic time, as you know."

"Torment and motivate?" Jon asked. "You'd make a great college counselor."

"We'll grab lunch next time, then," Phil said.

Draggin nodded, and Phil and Jon crossed the threshold to nachos and College Heaven.

Epilogue

"Mom! Mom!" a voice was shouting.

Michelle kept her eyes closed and pressed her eyes with her fingers, hoping the spinning feeling would stop.

"Mom! Are you OK?" the voice asked. Her son. Jack. She moved her hands from her eyes and opened them slowly.

"Jack?" Michelle asked.

"I heard a scream, and then I saw you on the floor," Jack said.

Michelle closed her eyes again. "Three fates… a dragon… on the Stairway," she said, her voice trailing off.

"Did you hit your head? Should I call an ambulance?" Jack asked.

Michelle took a deep breath, lifted her head up slowly from the backpack resting on the bottom step, and sat up. "The Stairway," she repeated.

"I'm calling 9-1-1," Jack said, pulling his cell phone out of his pocket.

"Jack," Michelle said. "Jack." She grabbed his hand and gave it a squeeze. "Jack, I'm fine. You told me about college, and I got nervous, and then I slipped going up the stairs, and… Ow! My ankle!"

"Are you OK?" Jack said. "Are you sure I shouldn't call an ambulance? At least let me get you some ice."

"I'm fine," Michelle said. "Ice would be great, yes, thank you." She caught sight of the college handout from Jack's school counselor and reached out her right hand to grab it. "And we're going to figure out this college thing, too."

"Don't worry about that right now," Jack said. "We can talk about college later," Jack said.

"Yes, later," Michelle said. An image of a purple dragon flashed across her mind, and she could almost hear Draggin's roar. "No! Let's talk about it now! We can't put it off any longer!"

"All right, all right, we can talk about it now, relax," Jack said. "I'll go get you some ice."

Michelle smiled. How bad could applying to college be? She focused her mind on the song playing on the radio in the kitchen. *But now it's time for me to go. The autumn moon lights my way...* She took a deep breath.

"Are you hungry, sweetie?" Michelle called over to Jack. "Let's talk about college stuff over dinner. I'm craving nachos."

– DRAGGIN'S COLLEGE PLANNING SCROLL –

Checklist

Today
- ☐ End your procrastination.

Sophomore Year

September
- ☐ Remind your child about taking the PSAT and/or PreACT.

December
- ☐ If your child achieves a score he is happy with on either the PSAT or the PreACT, arrange for him to take the corresponding official test, meaning either the SAT or ACT, at the end of the year or over the summer. If he didn't do well, start looking into Test Prep options.

January
- ☐ Do some career and major exploration together.
- ☐ Make sure your child applies to summer opportunities related to his college goals.
- ☐ Consult with a college counselor to discuss a possible future testing schedule for the SAT, ACT, and SAT Subject Tests.

March
- ☐ Register your child for any SAT Subject Tests that correspond well with the AP or other advanced courses he is taking.

April
- ☐ Finalize your child's summer activity plans.

May or June
- ☐ Obtain some classic or prizewinning literature for your child to read over the summer. Avid readers do very well in the college admissions process.
- ☐ Sign up your child for Test Prep if you haven't already started.
- ☐ Make sure your child takes any relevant SAT Subject Tests.

Junior Year

August
- ☐ Sign up your child for one fall SAT or ACT.

September
- ☐ Finalize your child's Test Prep strategy. Consult a college counselor, if you haven't already, to find out what's right for you.

October
- ☐ Remind your child about taking the PSAT / PreACT.

January
- ☐ Make plans for your child to take either the SAT or the ACT for a second time later in the school year based on the results of his first exam or October PSAT.
- ☐ Set aside time with your child to start creating a preliminary list of 20 colleges of interest.
- ☐ Help your child identify two 11th grade teachers of core academic subjects who can write strong Letters of Recommendation. Be sure your child goes above and beyond in their classes.
- ☐ Help your child generate a résumé.
- ☐ Make sure your child applies to summer opportunities related to his college goals.

February
- ☐ Plan campus visits for spring break and other upcoming long weekends. Be sure your child signs up for interviews wherever possible.
- ☐ Ensure your child gets on admissions offices' mailing lists and follows them on social media.

March

- ☐ Register your child for, and make sure he attends, upcoming spring College Fairs and/or local information sessions.
- ☐ Register your child for the April ACT or May SAT, and make sure he continues his Test Prep.
- ☐ Plan out with your child how to take on leadership roles next year, if he hasn't taken them on already.

April

- ☐ Register your child for the May or June SAT Subject Tests that correspond well with his AP, IB, or other advanced courses, and be sure he prepares.
- ☐ Continue to evaluate the College List with your child as you visit colleges and his test scores and/or GPA change.
- ☐ Finalize your child's summer activity plans.

May

- ☐ Be supportive while your child takes lots and lots of tests, including APs or IBs; the SAT or ACT; SAT Subject Tests; and, if he's a non-native English speaker, the TOEFL or IELTS.
- ☐ Make summer plans to visit colleges.

June

- ☐ Update your child's résumé together.
- ☐ Visit more colleges and arrange interviews when possible.
- ☐ Narrow down your child's list of schools, and divide them into Reach, Target, and Safety School options based on his SAT or ACT scores and his end-of-year academic record.
- ☐ Collect this year's essay prompts as they get released, and have your child work on as many essays as possible.
- ☐ Register your child for the July ACT, if available near you, or the August SAT/SAT Subject Tests, if needed, and make sure he continues his Test Prep.
- ☐ Find out the requirements for any art, music, or maker Portfolios, if your child is applying to art, music or engineering programs, or if he has a special talent in these areas. Your child should also work on putting these Portfolios together.

July

- ☐ Start your child on filling out the main portion of applications, including the Common Application, the Coalition Application, and any available school-specific or state applications.
- ☐ **July 4th (Independence Day) – This is your deadline for starting essays!**
- ☐ Support your child while he does an interesting summer activity.
- ☐ Set an end-of-month deadline to get his Main Essay done.

August

- ☐ August 1st - Get cracking! Most applications launch.
- ☐ Create the final and balanced College List, with three Reach, four Target, and three Safety Schools.
- ☐ Make sure your child writes as many Supplemental Essays as possible before the school year begins.
- ☐ Register your child for the September or the October SAT, SAT Subject Tests, and/or ACT, if needed. Don't forget to have him prepare.

Senior Year

September

- ☐ Urge your child to pick an Early Decision school, if desired.
- ☐ Identify which schools on your child's list offer Early Action so your child can meet those deadlines.
- ☐ Research all application and supplemental material deadlines for your child's schools. Sometimes Portfolios are due earlier than applications!
- ☐ **September 4th-ish (Labor Day) – This is the deadline for requesting Letters of Recommendation and completing any questionnaires or brag sheets that your child's Letter of Recommendation writers may require.**
- ☐ Have your child write more Supplemental Essays.
- ☐ Guide your child through more applications and any additional requested supporting materials.
- ☐ Remind your child to attend information sessions for colleges of interest at school and in the area.
- ☐ Continue to set up interviews and visit schools, if necessary.

October

- ☐ Use the testing agency websites to send your child's SAT, ACT, and/ or SAT Subject Tests scores to all Early Action or Early Decision schools.
- ☐ Complete financial aid forms, including the FAFSA and CSS Profile.
- ☐ Make sure your child is writing more Supplemental Essays.
- ☐ Finalize the Additional Information section together.
- ☐ Have your child fill out more applications.
- ☐ Review your child's résumé and have him update it one last time.
- ☐ Register for any remaining ACT, SAT, or SAT Subject Test attempts, and make sure that the Test Prep continues.
- ☐ Remind your child to attend information sessions for colleges of interest at school.
- ☐ Have your child follow up with his letter writers to make sure they've sent in their materials. Be sure he thanks them.
- ☐ October 14th - Be sure that your child submits any applications or materials with the October 15th early deadline.
- ☐ **October 31st (Halloween) – Make sure that your child submits all November 1st applications to avoid system crashes.**

November

- ☐ Have your child write more Supplemental Essays.
- ☐ Make sure your child fills out and submits more applications.
- ☐ Aim to submit at least one application per week.
- ☐ Rinse. Wash. Repeat. You're getting it now!

December

- ☐ Continue your support as your child works on whatever remains.
- ☐ Send his SAT, ACT, and/or SAT Subject Test scores to his Regular Decision schools.
- ☐ December 15th – Keep an eye out for those early application decisions.
- ☐ **December 31st (New Year's Eve) – Get your child to submit those last applications for any Regular Decision deadlines!**

January - May
- ☐ Recover and enjoy time with your friends and family.
- ☐ Watch your child's grades. They can go down a little bit, meaning a few As can become Bs, but they can't go down too much.
- ☐ Remind your child to stay out of trouble.

February
- ☐ **February 14th (Valentine's Day)** – This is your child's deadline for sending a loving update letter to all of the colleges that he's still waiting to hear from, including any from which he was deferred.

April
- ☐ **April 1st (April Fool's Day)** – Expect decisions from every college by this date.
- ☐ Compare financial aid packages.
- ☐ Get your child to Accepted Student Days so he can make one final visit to his options.

May
- ☐ **May 1st (May Day) - This is the deadline for your child to pick the college he will attend and submit his deposit.**

– DRAGGIN'S COLLEGE PLANNING SCROLL –
Glossary and Resources

TESTING

ACT. A standardized test that is an admissions requirement at many colleges. The ACT consists of the four required sections — English, Math, Reading, and Science — which are scored on a 1-36 point scale, and one optional Writing section, which is scored on a 2-12 point scale. Though students may opt out of the ACT Writing section, many colleges still require it, so always sign up for ACT with Writing. Students may instead take the SAT. For more information about the ACT, visit the ACT website (**act.org**).

Advanced Placement (AP) Tests. Exams offered in May that allow students to demonstrate achievement in particular subjects. Though not required for college admissions, AP Test scores can be a minor admissions factor. The tests are scored from 1-5, and some colleges give credit for scores of 3 or higher, though each school has its own policy for awarding credits. See International Baccalaureate as another example of college preparatory coursework.

College Board. The organization responsible for administering the SAT, PSAT, SAT Subject Tests, the AP Tests, and the CSS Profile.

International Baccalaureate (IB). An international educational program stressing global awareness, academic rigor, and breadth of knowledge. See Advanced Placement Tests as another example of college preparatory coursework.

International Baccalaureate (IB) Exams. Similar to AP Tests, these exams are offered in May and demonstrate achievement in particular subjects. Though not required for college admissions, predicted or actual IB Exam scores can be a minor admissions factor. The tests are offered at both higher level and standard level, and are scored from 1-7. Some colleges award credit for scores of 5 or higher on a higher-level exam, though each school has its own policy for awarding credits.

PreACT. A practice version of the ACT designed for sophomores.

PSAT/NMSQT. Preliminary SAT/National Merit Scholarship Qualifying Test. This annual October exam is designed as an opportunity for sophomores and juniors to practice for the SAT. The highest-scoring juniors, approximately the top one percent in each state, may qualify for the National Merit Scholarship or a merit scholarship sponsored by a college.

SAT. A standardized test developed by the College Board that is an admissions requirement at many colleges. The SAT consists of two required sections — Evidence-Based Reading and Writing (EBRW), and Math — which are each scored on a 200-800 point scale, along with one optional Essay section, which is scored on a 2-8 point scale. Though students may opt out of the SAT Essay section, many colleges still require it, so always sign up for the SAT with Writing. Students may instead take the ACT, the sworn enemy of the SAT. For more information about the SAT, visit the College Board website (**collegeboard.org**). For free SAT prep resources, visit the Khan Academy website (**khanacademy.org**).

SAT Subject Tests. Single-subject standardized tests that are sometimes admissions requirements, particularly for selective majors or colleges. They are one hour each and scored on a 200-800 point scale. For more information about the SAT Subject Tests, visit the College Board website (**collegeboard.org**). For practice tests, consider the College Board's book *The Official Study Guide for All SAT Subject Tests.*

Score Choice. An option offered by the College Board which allows students to send only SAT scores from specific test dates rather than all scores from all test dates. The ACT offers a similar option. Some colleges require all scores to be sent and, therefore, do not allow applicants to use Score Choice.

Superscore. The SAT or ACT score achieved by combining the highest section scores across multiple sittings (rather than using the section scores from only a single sitting). For example, suppose a student taking the SAT for the first time scores a 600 on Evidence-Based Reading and Writing and a 700 on Math, yielding a combined score of 1300. Suppose this student takes the SAT a second time and scores a 650 on Evidence-Based Reading and Writing and a 680 on Math, yielding a combined score of 1330. That student's Superscore would be 1350: the sum of the 700 on Math from the first sitting and the 650 on Evidence-Based Reading and Writing from the second sitting. Not all colleges Superscore.

Test Optional Colleges. Colleges that don't require the SAT or ACT. Really! For a list of colleges with flexible testing requirements, visit the FairTest website (**fairtest.org**).

Test Prep. Refers to any number of methods of coaching for standardized tests, particularly the SAT and ACT. The most common methods include group classes, private tutors, and online courses. Free SAT prep materials are available at the Khan Academy website (**khanacademy.org**).

COLLEGES

College List. The list of colleges to which a student is applying. A balanced College List typically consists of three Reach Schools, four Target Schools, and three Safety Schools.

CSS Profile. The financial aid form which students must often complete to apply for Institutional Financial Aid. To learn more about this form, visit the College Board's CSS Profile website (**cssprofile.collegeboard.org**).

Expected Family Contribution. Also known as "EFC." An estimate of the annual amount a family can contribute to college expenses. A family's EFC is calculated by a formula according to the information it enters in the FAFSA or the CSS Profile.

Free Application for Federal Student Aid. Also known as the "FAFSA." The form a student needs to complete to apply for Federal Financial Aid. Visit the FAFSA website (**fafsa.ed.gov**) to access this form, and google the term "fafsa4caster" to access a tool that will estimate your Federal Financial Aid.

Federal Financial Aid. Need-based financial aid from the US federal government. Federal Financial Aid can occur in the form of grants, loans, work-study, or any combination thereof.

Fit Factors. Factors beyond prestige that families should consider when building a College List. They include size, setting, academic offerings, academic climate, school culture, geography, and miscellaneous (the X-factor). To find colleges that have the Fit Factors that matter to your family, visit the College Board's Big Future website (**bigfuture.collegeboard. org**) and the Colleges That Change Lives website (**ctcl.org**), and browse Edward Fiske's book *Fiske Guide to Colleges* and Loren Pope's book *Colleges That Change Lives*.

Honors College / Honors Program. A special college or program within an institution designed for highly motivated and qualified students. Honors Colleges and Honors Programs may have separate Application Requirements and deadlines, and they often offer smaller class sizes, priority registration, separate housing, and Merit Aid. For more information about public Honors Colleges and Honors Programs, visit the Public University Honors website (**publicuniversityhonors.com**) or read John Willingham's book *Inside Honors*.

Hook. A student quality or experience so desirable to a college that it boosts the chances of admission. Hooks include, but are not limited to, being a member of the first generation in the family to graduate from college, being an underrepresented minority, demonstrating exceptional talent, being a recruited athlete, being a Legacy, donating huge sums of money to the school (seven figures!), or overcoming a very significant obstacle.

Institutional Financial Aid. Need-based or merit-based financial aid from a college's own funds (as opposed to from the US federal government).

Legacy. If an applicant's mom or dad has graduated from a certain college, then the applicant is a Legacy at that college. This is a common Hook.

Merit Aid. Financial aid awarded for merit rather than for financial need. Common examples of merit include a high GPA, a high ACT score, a high SAT score, or a special talent. Students are most likely to receive Merit Aid from private Safety Schools.

Net Price Calculator. A tool available on a college's website that helps prospective students estimate how much it will cost to attend the school after factoring in grants and scholarships. For more information about figuring out the cost of college, visit Lynn O'Shaughnessy's The College Solution website (**thecollegesolution.com**) and Mark Kantrowitz's FinAid website (**finaid.org**).

Reach School. A school with an acceptance rate below 25 percent or one for which an applicant's SAT or ACT score is below the 25th percentile for that school.

Safety School. A school with an acceptance rate above 25 percent for which an applicant's SAT or ACT score is above the 75th percentile for that school.

Target School. A school with an acceptance rate above 25 percent for which an applicant's SAT or ACT score is between the 25th percentile and the 75th percentile for that school.

Top 25 Schools. Also known as the "Top 25." The best 25 national universities as ranked by *U.S. News & World Report.* We also use the term as a shorthand for comparably selective liberal arts colleges, namely the "Top Ten National Liberal Arts Colleges" as ranked by *U.S. News & World Report.*

DEMONSTRATED INTEREST

College Fair. An event at which representatives from various colleges make themselves available to answer questions about their schools and to meet prospective applicants. Attending one is an opportunity to demonstrate interest.

Common Data Set. A publicly accessible standardized survey that many colleges complete every year. The Common Data Set is full of useful statistics, notably in Section C7, which includes the importance of various factors in the admissions process. For more information, visit the Common Data Set website (**commondataset.org**), or google "Common Data Set" and the name of the college that interests you.

Demonstrated Interest. Actions a student takes to show interest in a college. They include responding to marketing materials, signing up for email lists, following colleges on social media, cultivating relationships with admissions reps, visiting colleges, applying Early Action or Early Decision, and interviewing with the college. These actions are an admissions factor for many schools.

Early Action. Also referred to by some colleges as "Priority Deadline." A non-binding early application plan that requires students to submit applications earlier than the regular application deadline, typically no later than November 1st. Students may apply to more than one school Early

Action. Applying Early Action demonstrates interest and might improve chances for admission. Early Action notifications are usually sent out around December 15th.

Early Decision. A binding early application plan that requires students to submit applications earlier than the Regular Decision deadline, typically no later than November 1st. Students may apply to only one school Early Decision. A student applying Early Decision may still apply to multiple schools Early Action. Applying Early Decision demonstrates interest and might improve chances for admission. Early Decision notifications are usually sent out around December 15th.

Regular Decision. The traditional application plan for college admissions, as opposed to Early Action and Early Decision plans. Regular Decision deadlines typically fall between November and March, and a high concentration of them are around January 1st. Regular Decision notifications are sent out no later than April 1st.

Restrictive Early Action. Also referred to by some colleges as "Single-Choice Early Action." A non-binding early application plan that prohibits a student from applying Early Action or Early Decision to any other private school in the US. Applying Restrictive Early Action demonstrates interest and might improve chances for admission.

APPLICATIONS

Activities Section. The section of an application in which an applicant lists and briefly describes extracurricular activities. The Common App provides slots for ten activities, and the Coalition App provides slots for eight. To highlight the significance of their activities, students should use numbers ("raised $1,000" rather than "raised money") and action verbs (google "résumé action verbs"!).

Application Requirements. Refers to any or all of the following: the application form (including personal information, activities and awards, and essays); official score reports for the ACT, SAT, and/or SAT Subject Tests; official transcripts; Letters of Recommendation; interviews; and Portfolios.

Coalition Application. Also known as the "Coalition App." The Coalition App is an online application platform that was created in 2015 as an alternative to the Common App. Though the Coalition App has fewer member colleges than the Common App, the number of members is growing. To access this application, visit the Coalition App website (**mycoalition.org**).

Common Application. Also known as the "Common App." The Common App is an online application platform through which students can apply to many colleges. Most private colleges accept the Common App. To access this application, visit the Common App website (**commonapp.org**).

Honors and Awards Section. Also referred to in some application forms as the "Honors and Distinctions Section." The section of an application in which an applicant lists and briefly describes any honors, awards, or distinctions received. Both the Common App and Coalition App provide spaces for five.

Letter of Recommendation. Also known as a "Letter of Rec." A letter written by a teacher, counselor, or someone else who knows the student well enough to describe the student's academic gifts or personal qualities. Many colleges require two Letters of Recommendation from teachers of academic subjects and one from a counselor. Students should supply recommenders with a résumé and personal statement. Many recommenders also require students to complete an additional questionnaire.

Portfolio. A representative sample of the work of an applicant, particularly of an artist. The deadline for submitting a Portfolio to a college is sometimes earlier than the deadline for submitting the application to that college. Double check the dates! Many colleges require Portfolios to be submitted through the SlideRoom website (**slideroom.com**).

ESSAYS

Activity Essay. A common Supplemental Essay in which the applicant elaborates on the significance of an extracurricular activity. Rather than merely rehash an entry from the Activities Section of the application, this essay should provide details that give more insight into the applicant.

Additional Information Section. A section available on the Common Application, the Coalition Application, and other applications in which applicants may include any significant information that does not fit elsewhere in the application. This information may include family circumstances, health problems, explanations of bad grades, or anything else students think the colleges should know about them. Though optional, this section is the last chance to make sure no material information has been omitted.

Community Essay. A common Supplemental Essay in which the applicant explains her role within a community. The term community is open to interpretation; this essay can be an opportunity to explore identity, social causes, and interests. Schools want to know how applicants will contribute to their community and how applicants connect with the people around them.

Main Essay. Also known as the "personal statement," the "Common App essay," or the "application essay." Many colleges require some version of the Main Essay. Students are offered a choice of prompts, but all ask roughly the same question: "What is something important about you that we should know?"

Supplemental Essays. Required essays beyond the Main Essay. Supplemental Essays usually have word counts of around 250-300 words. The most common types include the Why This College Essay, the Community Essay, the Activity Essay, and the UC Essays. The Supplemental Essays should not repeat material from the Main Essay.

University of California Personal Insight Questions. Also known as the "UC Essays." Short essays required for admission to the University of California system. Students respond to four out of eight prompts. Unlike the Main Essay prompts, the University of California Personal Insight Questions should be answered directly with more emphasis on facts and less emphasis on storytelling.

Why This College Essay. A common Supplemental Essay in which the applicant explains why the college is a good fit for her or why the applicant is a good fit for the college. Effective answers typically include academic considerations, but professional goals, school culture, a strong extracurricular interest, and relevant past experiences can also be discussed. Applicants should avoid citing the beauty of the campus or college rankings as reasons to attend. Regardless of topic, the essay should be specific to the school.

About the Authors

Victoria

Victoria finished high school as Co-Valedictorian before she went on to earn her BA from Johns Hopkins University and her AM and PhD from Harvard University. Since then, she has worked on the faculties of Harvard University, Middlebury College's Italian School, and Elon University, before realizing that her true calling was college consulting. She now runs Distinctive College Consulting in Bethesda, Maryland. In her free time, however, she enjoys taking aimless walks around Washington, DC, reading and dancing with her daughter, and of course, eating nachos.

Phil

Phil graduated from Stanford, where he majored in English and minored in Human Biology. He enjoys playing basketball, tennis, boxing, social dancing, listening to podcasts, and visiting national parks. He lives in Silicon Valley where he dodges drones and electric self-driving cars on his skateboard and WRX. One day at Hot N Tot, Jon and Phil's diner of choice, Jon asked Phil if he wanted to start an educational counseling company, and thus was born Essaywise. The company has evolved over the years, but Phil still enjoys working with students and their families, and with Jon.

Jon

Jon has a BA in English from Stanford University and a JD from Harvard Law School. He supports Liverpool FC because their motto is, "You'll never walk alone." If you try to merge into Jon's lane, he will wave you over instead of accelerating and pretending he didn't see you. He lives with his wife and high school sweetheart (it's the same person, Jon is not a bigamist), and their two children, in Palos Verdes Estates, California. Jon and Phil offer a full range of college counseling services through Essaywise. If Jon is not spending time with his family or yours, he is probably playing soccer or chess.

Made in the USA
Lexington, KY
26 July 2018